Muṇḍaka Upaniṣad

Rediscovering Indian Literary Classics
(ISSN - 0972-0111)

1. Taittirīya Upaniṣad: With the Original Text in Sanskrit and Roman Transliteration. Translation with an Exhaustive Commentary; by Muni Narayana Prasad. (ISBN 81-246-0014-7)

2,4-5. Bṛhadāraṇyaka Upaniṣad: With Original Text in Roman Transliteration. English Translation and Appendices; by Nitya Chaitanya Yati; Vol. 1: Madhu Kāṇḍa; Vol. 2: Muni Kāṇḍa; Vol. 3: Khila Kāṇḍa. (ISBN 81-246-0008-2)

3. Kena Upaniṣad: With the Original Text in Sanskrit and Roman Transliteration. Translation with an Extensive Commentary; by Muni Narayana Prasad. (ISBN 81-246-0034-1)

6. Muṇḍaka Upaniṣad: With the Original Text in Sanskrit and Roman Transliteration. Translation with an Exhaustive Commentary; by Muni Narayana Prasad. (ISBN 81-246-0105-4)

7. Kaṭha Upaniṣad: With the Original Text in Sanskrit and Roman transliteration. Translation with an Exhaustive Commentary; by Muni Narayana Prasad. (ISBN 81-246-0110-0)

8. Praśna Upaniṣad: With the Original Text in Sanskrit and Roman transliteration. Translation with an Extensive Commentary; by Muni Narayana Prasad. (ISBN 81-246-0129-1)

9. Aitareya Upaniṣad: With the Original Text in Sanskrit and Roman transliteration. Translation with an Extensive Commentary; by Muni Narayana Prasad. (ISBN 81-246-0142-9)

10. Śrī Dakṣiṇāmūrti Stotram of Śrī Śaṅkarācārya; with the commentary Tattva Prakāśikā; by Swami Tattvavidananda Saraswati; Edited by Puppala B. (ISBN 81-246-0210-7)

11. Āditya Hṛdayam: With the Commentary Tattvaprakāśikā; by Swami Tattvavidananda Saraswati (ISBN 81-246-0231-X)

12. Vāstuśāstra: Ancient Indian Architecture and Civil Engineering — Retrospects and Prospects; by Rahul Kumar Altekar (ISBN 81-246-0246-8)

13. Gaṇapati Upaniṣad: With the Commentary Tattvaprakāśikā; by Swami Tattvavidananda Saraswati (ISBN 81-246-0265-4)

14. Life's Pilgrimage Through the Gītā; by Swami Muni Narayana Prasad (ISBN 81-246-310-3)

Rediscovering Indian Literary Classics, no. 6

Muṇḍaka Upaniṣad

With the original text in Sanskrit and Roman transliteration

Translation with
an Exhaustive Commentary
by

Swami Muni Narayana Prasad

D.K.Printworld (P) Ltd.
New Delhi

Cataloging in Publication Data — DK
[Courtesy: D.K. Agencies (P) Ltd. <docinfo@dkagencies.com>]

Narayana Prasad, *Muni*, 1938-
Muṇḍaka Upaniṣad : with the original text in Sanskrit and Roman transliteration ; translation with an exhaustive commentary by Swami Muni Narayana Prasad.
vii, 142 p., 23 cm.
(Rediscovering Indian literary classics; no. 6)
Includes bibliographical references (p.)
Includes glossary.
Includes index.
ISBN 8124601054

1. Upanishads. Muṇḍakopaniṣad — Commentaries. 2. Hinduism — Sacred books. 3. Hinduism — Rituals. I. Upaniṣads. Muṇḍakopaniṣad. English & Sanskrit. II. Title. III. Series: Rediscovering Indian literary classics; no. 6.

ISBN 81-246-0105-4
First published in India in 1998
Second impression in 2006

Published and printed by:
D.K. Printworld (P) Ltd.
Regd. office : *'Sri Kunj'*, F-52, Bali Nagar
New Delhi - 110 015
Phones : (011) 2545-3975; 2546-6019; *Fax* : (011) 2546-5926
E-mail: dkprintworld@vsnl.net
Web: www.dkprintworld.com

Preface

THE flower of Indian wisdom, the Upaniṣads reveal the Eternal Reality. Their teaching transcends the bounds of time and space. Their relevance to the age we live in becomes evident only when elucidated in a way that is natural to the thinking habits of this age. Most of the available commentaries on the Upaniṣads, are either those of masters who lived and taught centuries or even millennia ago, or are elucidations on those commentaries. A modern mind in search of the secret teaching, which the word *upaniṣad* implies, needs an interpretation of it in a form familiar to this age. It is this need that urged Guru Nitya Chaitanya Yati, Head of the Narayana Gurukula Foundation together with myself to take on the project of writing new commentaries on all the major ten Upaniṣads — he on the *Bṛhadāraṇyaka, Chāndogya,* and *Māṇḍūkya,* with myself on the rest. Guru Nitya's commentary on the *Bṛhadāraṇyaka* in three volumes is already published and the one on the *Chāndogya* is in the making. My commentaries on the *Kena* and *Taittirīya* are already in print and those on the *Kaṭha* and *Praśna* will follow. My *Īśa Upaniṣad* commentary has already appeared on a different format, as *The Basic Lessons on India's Wisdom.*

It is the philosophy of Sri Narayana Guru, a philosopher saint and the epicentre of a great social transformation in Southern India, who lived in the latter part of the last century, and the guidance that I received from his chief disciple and successor who is my own Guru — Nataraja Guru — that has enabled me to delve into at least some of the deeper aspects of the Upaniṣadic wisdom. My prostrations go to the feet of these two Gurus.

Unlike the other Upaniṣad commentaries, I happened to write the present one while living in an *āśrama* in the remote island state of Fiji in the South Pacific. Having no one else with whom to exchange ideas while writing, I have failed to offer sidelights on many issues that have since surfaced for discussion, which in the presence of other serious students would have been the case. This however was made amends for later in my commentary on the *Praśna Upaniṣad,* considered to be subsidiary to the *Muṇḍaka Upaniṣad,* which I wrote after reaching India on my return from Fiji, after having an open discussion on every minute aspect with a team of research scholars and seekers.

As in the case of the others, this commentary was also first written in my mother tongue, the Malayalam Language, which I translated afterwards into English. Mrs Sheilah Johns in England edited it simply out of her love for the wisdom of India. My gratitude to her is boundless.

The dissemination of ancient wisdom is greatly needed in our modern age to rescue it from its many imbalances. D.K. Printworld of New Delhi has taken on this need of the age as the soul of their business. It is on account of this passion that they bring out all these Upaniṣad commentaries.

This commentary may simply be regarded as the attempt of a modern mind to understand the ancient wisdom of India.

Jan. 14, 1998 **Swami Muni Narayana Prasad**

Contents

Introduction

THE Upaniṣads form the basic texts of Indian wisdom. Are they religious scriptures, or simply outpourings of philosophical visions? To answer this question we need to equip ourselves with a clear notion of the core of what makes a religion a religion.

A religion as such is marked by certain basic tenets it believes in, based on which its entire edifice is erected. A Christian, for example, has to believe that Jesus was the son of God, that he underwent the vicarious suffering of crucifixion out of his love for the human race in order to save it from the original sin, and that he bodily ascended into heaven on the third day after he was buried. Likewise, Islam too has its basic tenets — that none but Allah is adorable and that Mohammad was his last messenger. Do the Upaniṣads insist on any such inviolable basic tenet? No. They enjoin us instead to closely observe the world we live in, our life, its changefulness and activities, and to know the Truth — the unchanging Reality — underlying all. If unable to discover that Reality on one's own, one will have to get the guidance of a Master — a *guru*, an enlightened one — by approaching him with full faith (*śraddhā*) and asking him relevant questions. Realizing the one Supreme Reality, either on one's own or with the help of a Master, is what makes life fully fruitful and what man needs finally to attain. Such in general is the nature of the Upaniṣadic message, the *Muṇḍaka Upaniṣad* being no exception. Thus basically the Upaniṣads are different expressions of the one vision of the one Reality. The *ṛṣi*s, when they uttered these words of vision, were not inspired by the zeal of a religious missionary or of a messenger of God, or even that of the propounder of a new vision. Countless are the ways the one Reality is visualizable, as each Upaniṣad manifests.

What Indian thought, particularly Vedānta, has in it in the place of dogmatic belief in religions is *śraddhā*, itself translatable as 'belief'.

Śraddhā, a seeker's undoubting belief in the veracity of the words of instruction of his immediate *guru* as also in those of former masters recorded in texts like the Upaniṣads, is quite unlike any religious dogma. It is merely an attitude a seeker develops towards his *guru*. It is absolutely essential for the seeker to realize the Reality on his own, through his intense cogitation and meditation. That which is to be cogitated on and meditated upon is provided initially by the *guru*, the realized person. His assurance and initial instruction on the final certitude are accepted by the seeker in full faith. Such instruction may contain even the final words of wisdom teaching such as *tat-tvam-asi* (That Thou Art), still remaining mere words good to be believed in, for the seeker. Only on attaining the final enlightenment on his own does he become convinced of the veracity of such words, which until and unless realized thus are a matter of mere belief for him. Once realized, it is no more a belief but an accomplished fact. Yet that accomplishment was possible only because he believed in it initially, which led him to cogitate on it and to meditate, and on attainment, fully satisfied, he congratulates himself for initially believing in those words. Being such, *śraddhā* is no dogmatic belief. By this simple belief in the guidance given by an accomplished Master, the seeker is provided with a firm base whence to begin his journey so that the end result would also be certain. Fully enlightened as to what Reality is, he no longer feels the need for any belief. *Muṇḍaka* is an Upaniṣad that gives much emphasis to the *śraddhā* aspect.

This Upaniṣad begins by depicting a line of *guru*s who handed down this wisdom of *Brahman*. The first mentioned is Brahmā, the Creator himself, showing the beginninglessness of this wisdom. This Upaniṣad presents the wisdom as taught by Aṅgiras, who belonged to this line of *guru*s, to Śaunaka.

Śaunaka asks Aṅgiras, "Venerable Sir, knowing what does all this world become known?" The answer to this one question is a long discourse that runs to three *Muṇḍaka*s (chapters), each having two *khaṇḍa*s (sections).

The culmination of this teaching concerns the experiential awareness Śaunaka is all set to attain: "The knower of the Transcendental *Brahman* becomes *Brahman* indeed. In his line is never born a non-*Brahman*-knower. He, crossing over sorrows, crossing over sins, becomes freed from all knots in the heart. He becomes Immortal. " Śaunaka, at first a seeker, thus finally attains certitude, and between these two extremes comes the body of the teaching.

This wisdom in its pristine form, all admit, is upheld by the *saṁnyāsins* (renunciate monks) of India, and the philosophical teaching for their life-pattern is provided by the Upaniṣads. Yet occasions that emphasize the need for such a way of life hardly ever appear in them, *Muṇḍaka Upaniṣad* being an exception. *Saṁnyāsins*, for this reason, treat this Upaniṣad as of especial importance as the scriptural authority for their way of life, the very name of it suggesting shaving off one's hair (*muṇḍaka*). Besides, passages such as *saṁnyāsa-yogād yatayaḥ śuddha-sattvāḥ* (those of self-restraint, through the *yoga* of renunciation or *saṁnyāsa*, attain pure beingness) (III.ii.6) and *bhaikṣacaryam carantaḥ* (living on alms) (I.ii.11) exalt the *saṁnyāsins*' way of life.

That it is in *saṁnyāsins* that, as a rule, *Brahman*-wisdom attains to perfection is the general stance preferred by this Upaniṣad, perhaps because it is one that is appended to the *Atharvaveda*, the one Veda which exalts non-hedonistic values, an attitude more natural to the pre-Vedic culture of India than to Vedism.

Yet another peculiarity that separates this Upaniṣad from others is the way in which it denounces Vedic ritualism. Section 2 of *Muṇḍaka* I, highlights the defects and weak points of Vedism and its ritual, and advises the seeker to become indifferent to them and to consider a renunciate's life as ideal. The other Upaniṣads, on the other hand, prefer to get over Vedism by drowning its already existing concepts of limited hedonistic sense and value, in the all-inclusive universal sense and value, acceptable to the new wisdom of Vedānta, given to the very same concepts — an indirect way of correcting and revising the former in the light of the latter.

Knowledge, in the first chapter (*Muṇḍaka*) of this Upaniṣad, is categorized as *parā-vidyā* and *aparā-vidyā* (transcendental and non-transcendental knowledge), as a systematic beginning of the search for Reality. Everything in this world, the seeker not excluded, emerges from *Brahman*, the one and only Reality, as a result of the *tapas* (self-heating) for self-unfoldment it undergoes (Verse I.i.8). The seeker's yearning for Reality is nothing but his aspiration to search for his own original source. This aspect only becomes explicit as we reach the last chapter (*Muṇḍaka* III).

Aparā-vidyā, ritualism being its most glaring example, is denounced all through the second section of the first chapter. One who gets past the tangled ritualism to the world of *parā-vidyā*'s clarity approaches a proper *guru*, serves him, and asks him vital, relevant questions that assist him in the solution of his basic problems. Śaunaka, the seeker of the present Upaniṣad, was also a ritualist householder (*mahā-śāla*) who intently changed over to the wisdom's way.

Chapter II, in its first section, makes it clear how *Brahman* is the one Causal Reality, and in the second, reveals the way to get to know that Reality.

How *Brahman* is a mystical experience, and how full of contradictions it is when considered logically,are laid bare in the first section of *Muṇḍaka* III. Its second section elucidates as to who can be eligible for the knowledge of that Reality, how to equip oneself for that attainment, and what the nature of that ultimate attainment is.

Learning an Upaniṣad, going deep into all its implications, does not make one a self-realized person. Had it been so all the expounders of scriptures would have been such. But it is not so. The actual life lived by those who expound such teachings and the essence of what they teach mostly remain oceans apart, sometimes even making a mockery of the selfsame teaching. That what the Upaniṣads teach has to be realized in our actual life, in the here and now, or else it would be a waste of life, as the *Kena Upaniṣad* (II.5) says, is insisted on by almost all of them.

The words of the Upaniṣads, of deep significance though they are, therefore, are mere alluring wrappings within which is concealed the real secret, yet to be uncovered. It has to be unwrapped; only then one sees the precious Reality hidden within. This uncovering the seeker has to do on his own, and this is where the loving guidance of a *guru* is actually needed. The *Īśa Upaniṣad* poignantly strikes at this point, after expounding Reality as well as could be done through words, as follows:

Concealed in a golden casket is Reality's face,

Uncover it, O Pūṣan, for me, the lover of living
Truth to perceive.

This commentary on the *Muṇḍaka Upaniṣad*, therefore, does not unveil the secret teaching therein but is meant to be considered as a mere aid to one's own cogitation and meditation on attaining wisdom's ineffable core.

ॐ भद्रं कर्णेभिः शृणुयाम देवा।
भद्रं पश्येमाक्षभिर्यजत्राः ।
स्थिरैरङ्गैस्तुष्टुवाँ सस्तनूभिर्
व्यशेम देवहितं यदायुः।।
स्वस्ति न इन्द्रो वृद्धश्रवाः
स्वस्ति नः पूषा विश्ववेदाः।
स्वस्ति नस्तार्क्ष्यो अरिष्टनेमिः
स्वस्ति नो बृहस्पतिर्दधातु।।

ॐ शान्तिः शान्तिः शान्तिः

Om bhadram karṇebhiḥ sṛṇuyāma devā
bhadram paśyema akṣabhir yajatrāḥ ।
sthirair aṅgais tuṣṭuvāṁsaḥ tanūbhir-
vyaśema devahitam yad āyaḥ ।।

svasti na indro vṛddhaśravāḥ
svasti naḥ pūṣā viśvavedāḥ ।
svasti nas tārkṣyo ariṣṭanemiḥ
svasti no bṛhaspatir dadhātu ।।

oṁ śāntiḥ śantiḥ śāntiḥ

The auspicious, o gods, may we hear with our ears;
The auspicious may we, the maintainers
The god-given duration of life, may we occupy with bodies strong of limbs.
May Indra of nature learning bless us with well- being;
May Pūṣan, the all-knower, bless us with well living;
May Tārkṣya (Garuḍa) of unobstructed circumferential path, bless us with well-being;
May Bṛhaspati bless us with well-being.

Om Peace! Peace! Peace!

MUṆḌAKA I

KHAṆḌA 1

ॐ ब्रह्मा देवानां प्रथमः सम्बभूव विश्वस्य कर्ता भुवनस्य गोप्ता।
स ब्रह्मविद्यां सर्वविद्याप्रतिष्ठामथर्वाय ज्येष्ठपुत्राय प्राह ॥ १ ॥

oṁ brahmā devānāṁ prathamaḥ sambabhūva
viśvasya kartā bhuvanasya goptā ।
sa brahmavidyāṁ sarvavidyāpratiṣṭhām
atharvāya jyeṣṭhaputrāya prāha ॥ 1 ॥

Brahmā, the creator of all and the sustainer of the world, emerged as the first of gods. He taught the science of *Brahman* (*brahmavidyā*), the basis of all sciences, to Atharvān, his eldest son.

India's culture, ancient as it is, has its own time-honoured concept of arts (*kalā*) and sciences (*vidyā*). The former, divisible as aesthetic and utility arts (*hṛdya-kalā* and *upajīvana-kalā*), are sixty-four in number and the latter, eighteen. Each branch of science, each branch of art, has its own source book, each beginning with the rather odd claim: the origin of this science has come from Brahmā the Creator who taught it first to so-and-so. The implication is: the particular science or art is as old and exalted as the world is, and it has reached us as handed down from generation to generation. That man's thinking and innovating habit is as old as the world and that both originated from one and the same source are also signified by this otherwise seemingly ostentatious claim. The primeval source of the world is the primeval source of all sciences too.

Consciousness One, Sciences Many

Pursuing each science, our mind is made to work in a different way, each pursuit resulting in the gain of a different knowledge. The fact that it is one mind, one consciousness, that functions in different ways dealing with different subjects and acquiring, or rather transforming itself into, different kinds of knowledge, goes into oblivion while we think. One and the same consciousness is at the basis of all sciences, which conciousness is none other than the primeval source not only of all sciences but also of all the worlds.

The science of our concern here is *Brahmavidyā*, the science of the Absolute, the science that claims to be the basis of all sciences. Each science being a specific mode of function of one *cit* (consciousness) with a specific object or field of interest, all science has one *cit* as its source. To have a vivid awareness of this basic consciousness is thus in effect to know the basis of all sciences and in that sense is equivalent to knowing all sciences. *Brahman* being the all-abiding substance, Pure Consciousness in essence, Its science turns out to be the Science of all sciences.

Brahmavidyā and Ātmavidyā

One and boundless, the *cit* is experienced by each of us as *my* consciousness as though divisible and many. Examining the ambit of *my* own consciousness what I realize is that there is nothing beyond its bounds. Everything knowable or imaginable is within it. Even that which is supposedly outside its scope is *understood* to be so; everything *understood* being within consciousness, it is therefore within it. The boubdless *cit* could well be compared to a circle that has infinity as its circumference.

Around a point could be drawn any number of circles, each outer circle larger than the inner ones. Infinity is the limit whereto such circles could be enlarged, reaching which the centre loses its centrality as the circle that has infinity for circumference can have any point within it for its centre. That is to say,whilst the circle remains one, its centre could be as many as infinity. Virtually each one of us is one of those centres. I feel I am the centre of that infinite circle. You feel you are the centre. Oneself is the centre of the universe for each of us, a feeling wrong in no way, but not right in any way. This feeling in no way affects the oneness, boundlessness and indivisibility of the one circle, the one Consciousness, *cit*.

This one Consciousness, one infinite circle, perceived circumference-wise is called *Brahman*, and knowing it thus-wise is *Brahmavidyā* (the science of the Absolute). Perceived from the centre, this same Consciousness is called *ātman* (the Self), and knowing it thus is *ātmavidyā* (the science of the Self). This knowledge is known as *Brahmavidyā*, also in the sense that it was first taught by Brahmā, the Creator, as Śaṅkara suggests in his commentary.

A Hierarchy of Gurus

Some sciences, as the custom has always been, would be taught by its adepts only to the fully competent and aspiring; or else they would keep it a secret. This custom strangely prevails even today, especially in sciences like Indian medicine where exceptionally rare ways of treating unusual cases are necessitated. All the more meaningful is the importance given to this custom in the case of *Brahmavidyā*. A Master, a *guru*, teaches a seeker, a *śiṣya*, only on becoming fully convinced of the latter's unrelenting quest for wisdom and his competence for it. Brahmā, the original Master of this wisdom, according to the present Upaniṣad, first taught it to his son Atharvān; son in the wisdom context also meaning disciple, the eldest son could be the first disciple. Why this wisdom is a secret and why is it taught only to chosen disciples will become evident as we proceed.

Etymologically meaning that which grows unceasingly, the word *Brahman* is used in two senses: as masculine gender it signifies the Creator and as neuter the Absolute, the all-abiding Reality. Both the usages appear in this one stanza. That the Creator of the world himself is the originator of the wisdom taught here suggests that it was not authored, discovered or proposed by any particular individual as is the case with theories like Cartesianism, Kantianism, Hegelianism, Newtonianism and so on. With no proponent of its own, this wisdom has always been in the human world ever since its beginning, if indeed it had any. It is the wisdom that underlies the origin and existence of the world and life. It is in the very same sense that the Vedas, the four basic scriptures of India, are considered to be of non-human origin (*apauruṣeya*).

In certain cases, it is to be conceded, the names of particular *ṛṣis* are attached to particular philosophies, as for example, Patañjali's Yoga system, Kapila's Sāṁkhya system, Kaṇāda's Vaiśeṣika system. Yet when examined closely it becomes evident that the particular *ṛṣi* does not claim to be the proponent of the system; he was simply codifying the scattered ideas already existing, into a well-structured system of thought. The *ṛṣi* would not say who the originator of the line of thought was, feeling it better to leave it unknown. He would say, "We have heard so from our predecessors", or "There is this verse concerning it", or something along similar lines.

अथर्वणे यां प्रवदेत ब्रह्माऽथर्वा तां पुरोवाचाङ्गिरे ब्रह्मविद्याम् ।
स भारद्वाजाय सत्यवहाय प्राह भारद्वाजोऽङ्गिरसे परावराम् ।। २ ।।

atharvaṇe yāṁ pravadeta brahmā'tharvā
tāṁ purovācāṅgire brahmavidyām ।
sa bhāradvājāya satyavahāya prāha
bhāradvājo'aṅgirase parāvarām ।। 2 ।।

What Brahmā imparted to Atharvān,
Even that science of *Brahman*
Atharvān taught to Aṅgira in olden days;
He in turn taught it to Satyavaha of the Bharadvāja clan;
And Bhāradvāja (Satyavaha) imparted
This hierarchical wisdom to Aṅgiras.

The wisdom as old as the world, *Brahmavidyā*, in order to be revealed in its wholeness to humanity, needs Masters who are its embodiments and who willingly impart it to earnest seekers. As the basis of all sciences, its guiding light is most needed in all realms of human life to make it well-balanced and well-founded. The Masters of this wisdom, called *gurus*, for this reason, have always been adored everywhere, and their long line paid homage to.

The line of *gurus* beginning with Brahmā and coming down through

Atharvān, Angira, Satyavaha, and Aṅgiras is only one of many such lines that have cropped up in the long history of mankind. A fully dedicated and self-withdrawn life being natural with such Masters, their imparting of wisdom often gained the complexion of a religious movement, each of such movement recognizing a particular line of Masters.

The Advaita School, with Śaṅkara for its promulgator, recognizes another line of *guru*s originating from Nārāyaṇa, the all-sustaining Viṣṇu himself. It comes down through Padmabhava (the lotus-born Brahmā), Vasiṣṭha, Śakti, Parāśara, Vyāsa, Śuka, Gauḍapāda, Govinda, Śaṅkara, Padmapāda, Hastāmalaka,Toṭaka, followed by a line of further elucidators of the Advaita philosophy. All these *guru*s are formally paid homage to by all the seekers. Often it is simply stated in short, "We pay homage to the hierarchy of *guru*s that began with Nārāyaṇa and, with Śaṅkara in the middle, lasted till our own *guru*."

शौनको ह वै महाशालोऽङ्गिरसं विधिवदुपसन्नः पप्रच्छ।
कस्मिन्नु भगवो विज्ञाते सर्वमिदं विज्ञातं भवतीति।। ३।।

śaunako, ha vai mahāśālo'ṅgirasaṁ
vidhivad upasannaḥ papraccha ।
kasminnu bhagavo vijñāte
sarvam idaṁvi jñātaṁ bhavatīti ।। 3 ।।

Śaunaka, the great householder,
approaching Aṅgiras as enjoined, asked:
"Venerable Sir, knowing what
does all this world become known?"

The Great Householder

With the nature of wisdom-teaching of this Upaniṣad in view, the seeker being a householder is of special significance. The teaching at the very outset delineates what is deficient in ritualism — what is known as *karma-mārga*, the path of actions — and how the way of wisdom (*jñāna-mārga*) is free of all such failings. The actual wisdom teaching follows it. Ritualists in the normal course are householders.

always bound by worldly obligations that urge them to be engaged in activities (*karmas*). Finding themselves thus bound, they search for means to free themselves which (in turn) they find in religious rituals, propitiatiory or entreating. Such rituals, also actions (*karmas*) intended for particular results, often of decisive concern, in effect bind them to more actions instead of freeing them — a vicious circle they are trapped in by their own ignorance. Their understanding of life, their interests in life, are all confined to the limits of closed circles, say of their own family, business, friends, relatives, merry-making and the like, never rising up to perceive 'all the world' (*sarvam idam*) while thinking of life. They, for this reason, fail to become aware of an all-sustaining substance, the one meaning of all life. To save such people from the predicament they are in, by imparting the wisdom of *Brahman,* is the purport of this Upaniṣad. Given these, a great householder, representing all ritualists, becoming a seeker is highly symbolic in significance.

The interest of the present householder, as is evident from his question, has diverted from closed circles to 'all this world'. That the Reality is to be viewed from the all inclusive perspective of 'all the worlds' and not from the perspective of personal existence and personal interests, he is aware of. As is implied in the question, "Knowing what all this world becomes known?" he must have heard of this wisdom from someone somehow, yet is in the dark as to what it is and how to attain it. Householders hardly turn to such an enquiry unless they come face to face with some insoluble difficulties or conflicting situations in life, making them doubt if life has any meaning at all.

Peculiarity of the Question

The question Śaunaka asks is a direct one, entering right into the problem of *Brahmavidyā*, with no reference to any impending life problem to be solved and no dramatic situation created to make the teaching imminent. What he is in search of is the science that serves as basis for all sciences. Almost the same is the question asked by Āruṇi of the *Chāndogya Upaniṣad* to his son Śvetaketu on his returning home from the *gurukula* (forest school), greatly conceited on formally completing his education. The father asks him:

> You seem to be greatly conceited and arrogant, and think yourself well read. Well, did you ask your teacher for that

> teaching by which the unhearable becomes heard, the unperceivable becomes perceived, the unknowable becomes known? (VI.i.2-3)

A humiliated Śvetaketu admits his ignorance and requests his father to teach him that wisdom. Āruṇi begins by saying:

> Just as, my dear, by knowing one gold
> ornament everything made of gold
> becomes known; distinct modes
> being only names arising from speech,
> while the truth is that it is just gold.
>
> (VI-i. 5)

As Enjoined

That Śaunaka's approaching Aṅgiras was 'as enjoined' is mentioned as though underscored. Scriptures and custom prescribe certain ways in which a seeker should approach a master, yet no details of it are given here. Stanza 12 of the next section that follows indicates that the disciple should be carrying a bundle of sacrificial fuel (*samit-pāṇiḥ*), the implication of which we'd better discuss later. That the way in which a seeker approaches should be indicative of his intention, his relentless quest for wisdom, dedication, faith, devoutness and the like, is what is significant. While fulfilling such traditional customs his mind should get filled with the satisfaction of having imbibed the implied meanings of the custom, not with the self-appreciation of fulfilling a prescribed approach.

Śaṅkara, is his commentary, raises the question whether this particular custom began with Śaunaka's approaching Aṅgiras, or was prevailing even prior to this. He answers it by comparing Śaunaka's doing so to a lamp lit at the threshold of a building; it sheds light both inside and outside. So too Śaunaka's abiding with the custom refers both backwards and forwards. As is to be presumed from this explanation of Śaṅkara, he considers Śaunaka's approaching Aṅgiras and asking the most fundamental of all questions as a sort of threshold to the history of the devlopment of Indian thought. A tacit understanding as to how a disciple should approach a *guru* must have been there even before this

Upaniṣadic incident, but no specific reference to it is available in any of the scriptures prior to the present one.

तस्मै स होवाच । द्वे विद्ये वेदितव्ये इति ह स्म
यद् ब्रह्मविदो वदन्ति, परा चैवापरा च ॥ ४ ॥

tasmai sa hovāca — dve vidye veditavye iti ha sma
yad brahmavido vadanti, parā caivāparā ca ॥ 4 ॥

To him then he said:
Two kinds of knowledge are there to know,
As indeed *Brahman*-knowers are wont to say:
The transcendental (*parā*) and the immanent (*aparā*).

Categorizing the entire range of knowledge into two is all that is done in this stanza, all its details to follow. Śaṅkara, in his commentary, raises an objection and answers it himself: The seeker's request was for the teaching of a particular science whereas the master begins to answer with the entire range of knowledge in view. The answer therefore is not to the point. Śaṅkara replies to this objection thus: though it is a particular science that is requisitioned to be taught, the peculiarity of that science is that it forms the basis of all sciences. Knowing *that* science, knowing the science of consciousness that unfolds itself as all sciences, is different from getting familiarized with a particular science. To make clear how *this* science is different, comparing its scope with those of various other sciences is a necessity.

Meaningful only to those who are seeking the knowledge of the whole of existence and not to others who are after piecemeal knowledge of worldly benefits, the two categories, following the Vedic background, to which all the Upaniṣads belong, are named *parā* and *aparā*. The same, in the modern age, is named by Narayana Guru in his *Ātmopadeśa-śatakam* (One Hundred Verses of Self-Instruction) as *sama* (literally 'the same') and *anya* ('the other'), based on how the mind functions on knowing. Knowing every entity distinctly is named *anya*; perceiving all as experiences, ideas, images, and so on getting formulated in the one and only field of consciousness or rather mind, and so not different in essential content, is named *sama*. The *parā* of the present Upaniṣad corresponds to the *sama* of Narayana Guru's classification, and *aparā* to his *anya*. Every particular life-experience or knowledge is perceivable as "This is an aspect of knowledge","This is yet another aspect of knowledge" and so on, all thus converging into the one knowledge. Do meditate on what is signified by 'this' in the statement 'This is knowledge'. This meditation leads the seeker to the realization of the one Reality in all appearances. Such is the way Narayana Guru, with his modern outlook, guides the seeker by making use of the *sama-anya* classification. So too, concentrating on the 'this' of "This is *parā*-consciousness" one would attain to the non-dual Reality.

This classification of knowledge, made merely by way of preparing the ground for the ensuing teaching, is somewhat comparable to showing the scope of the field of enquiry and then delimitting it to some particular aspect of it before serious research work is begun in modern academic studies. The peculiarity of the delimited field in the present case is that it, the scope of the reality it searches for, subsumes the entirety of all the fields of human interest, making of it the basis of all sciences, the Science of all sciences. Appreciating the glory of that Science must needs be preceded by an overall view of the entire field of human interests and enquiry, as is achieved by the present verse.

तत्रापरा, ऋग्वेदो यजुर्वेदः सामवेदोऽथर्ववेदः शिक्षा कल्पो व्याकरणं निरुक्तं
छन्दो ज्योतिषमिति । अथ परा, यया तदक्षरमधिगम्यते ॥ ५ ॥

tatrāparā, ṛgvedo yajurvedaḥ sāmavedo atharvavedaḥ
śikṣā kalpo vyākaraṇaṁ niruktaṁ chando jyotiṣamiti ।
atha parā, yayā tad akṣaram adhigamyate ॥ 5 ॥

Of these, the immanent consists of the *Ṛgveda, Yajurveda, Sāmaveda* and *Atharvaveda*; Pronuncation (*śikṣā*), Ritual (*kalpa*), Grammar (*vyākaraṇam*), Etymology (*niruktam*), Metrics (*chandas*) and Astrology (*jyotiṣam*). And the transcendental is that whereby the Imperishable is comprehended.

The ancient culture of India was Veda-centred, and its system of education was therefore Veda-centred likewise. One well versed in the Vedas was considered well-educated. Vedism urges its adherents to strictly follow the path of rituals even to ensure worldly gains. It is on the ground of such a worldly-minded Vedic ritualism that the new seed of the culture of Vedānta sprouted and grew up as the most beautiful and most fruitful tree of wisdom proffering its sweetness to anyone anywhere in the world. The Upaniṣads in general, for this reason, treat Vedic rituals, as also the Vedas, as the background against which is set their wisdom in full contrast. Treating all the four Vedas and their subsidiaries as representing worldly knowledge, and thus as constituting the immanent knowledge, is thereby understandable. This Upaniṣad, in its next section, will slight the Vedic rituals, urging us to pass over their narrow-mindedness and restrictions, to reach out to the Freedom the transcendental Wisdom represents.

Strictly true to the Vedic background, only the Vedas and their subsidiary disciplines are mentioned here as pertaining to immanent knowledge. A wider range that brings in almost all the disciplines known at the time of its composition, is portryed in the *Chāndogya Upaniṣad* (Chapter VII) where Nārada as a seeker approaches Sanatkumāra for higher wisdom. The latter asks: "Tell me all that you know so that I can teach you what you do not know but you ought to know." Nārada enumerates all the sciences he knew: The *Ṛgveda, Yajurveda, Sāmaveda, Atharvaveda,* Epics (*itihāsas*), Mythological Legends (*Purāṇas*), Grammar, the science of ancestral worship (*piṭr vidyā*), Mathematics, Theology, Economics, Logic, Ethics, the science of *Brahman* (*Brahmavidyā*), Physical Science, the science of warfare, Astronomy, Fine Arts. Though knowing all the known sciences, he feels he is the knower only of the verbal aspect of all of them (*mantra-vit*), and not the knower of their Self (*ātma-vit*). Even the science of *Brahman* he knew was merely verbal knowledge. *Mantra-vit* (literally, the knower of *mantras*, the knower of meditatable words) is the one who has learnt the basic textbooks. But the full satisfaction of having learnt a science arises only when one becomes *ātma-vit*, that is to say, when one discovers any science, any knowledge, any experience, as the self-expression of the one Reality, the Self-Reality, and thus as not apart from self-reality or from oneself. Nārada's objective was to become an *ātma-vit* (literally, the knower of the Self). What is differentiated as *parā-vidyā* and *aparā-vidyā* in the present Upaniṣad and as *ātmā-vit* and *mantra-vit* in the *Chāndogya Upaniṣad* signifies the same in essence.

Though each of the four Vedas has in it the *Saṁhitā* section praising gods and dealing with rituals, the *Brāhmaṇa* and *Āraṇyaka* sections, both elaborations on the ritual aspects, and the *Upaniṣad*s expounding pure wisdom, the word *veda* is normally used only to denote the *Saṁhitā* part. And in that sense *aparā-vidyā* is the familiarity with the *Saṁhitā* part and the rituals expounded in the *Brāhmaṇa*s and *Araṇyaka*s, the three together known as *karma-kāṇḍa* (the section dealing with actions or rituals). The Upaniṣads and their wisdom, known also as *jñāna-kāṇḍa* (section dealing with wisdom), then form the *parā-vidyā*. The word *veda*, in a broader sense, signifies all the four sections together; and in that case, learning their literal sense is *aparā-vidyā*, and making one's own the mystico-philosophical vision concealed in those words is *parā-vidyā*. Realizing it, one finds one's oneness with the Reality realized, and is thus Self-realized (*ātma-vit*). Not merely a gaining of knowledge of something called Reality, it is the experience of the self-contentment and self-fulfilment of having attained that which is finally to be attained in life. The Reality thus realized is imperishable (*akṣaram*) as is made more explicit in the next verse.

यत् तदद्रेश्यमग्राह्यमगोत्रमवर्णमचक्षुःश्रोत्रं तदपाणिपादम् ।
नित्यं विभुं सर्वगतं सुसूक्ष्मं तदव्ययं यद् भूतयोनिं परिपश्यन्ति धीराः ॥ ६ ॥

yat tad-adreśyam agrāhyam agotram avarṇam
acakṣuḥ-śrotraṁ tad-apāṇi-pādam ।
nityaṁ vibhuṁ sarvagataṁ susūkṣmaṁ
tada-avyayaṁ yad bhūtayoniṁ paripaśyanti dhīrāḥ ॥6॥

Invisible, ungraspable, having no family line, colourless, sightless, hearingless, it is, the handless and feetless.
Eternal, omnipresent, all-pervading,
Exceedingly subtle that undecaying is,
Perceived all over by the wise
As the source of all that has emerged.

That the Imperishable mentioned in the last verse is the original source-substance (*yoni*) of all that has come into being (*bhūta*) in this world and as this world, is what is spotlighted in the present verse, pointing out what It is not in the first half and then what It is in the second.

The preconception that matter is the causal source of all that is is the basis of all modern scientific enquiry, even as the belief that God is the causal source of all in religions; though neither is provable nor disprovable. The perception of modern science in this respect is in no way more credible than the religious beliefs. Nevertheless, admitting the unknowability of the source Reality, God, makes religion all the more respectable owing to this honesty.

Matter, not admitted by modern science as an unknown matter, is energy in essence. Invisible though, energy quite mysteriously assumes the visible forms of everything in the universe. The Vedāntin's concept of the source, on the other hand, is not merely of objective appearances; it is also the source of the subject, the knower. The undecaying Substance understood here is thus the invisible and unknowable Reality that emerges as all that appears to be, the knowables as well as the knowing mind.

Matter is defined as that which has mass and occupies space. What we know of matter thus are two of its distinguishing or rather defining qualities, that which is quilified, the matter, yet remaining unknown. Science does not answer the question, "What is that substance that has mass and occupies space?" Divested of such qualities matter becomes non-matter, even unthinkable. Form, for example, is a quality of gross matter. Divested of this quality, matter is formless and thus invisible. Even energy, the constituent of matter, as all of us know, is invisible. So, strictly speaking, the source of all appearance, even as modern science conceives it, is invisible.

The Undecaying

The undecaying source of everything could well be understood with the help of the analogy of the gold ornament of the *Chāndogya Upaniṣad* (VI. i. 5). A piece of ornament is made of gold, i.e., gold is the substance in the visible form of ornament. Ornament is merely a momentary form assumed by gold. Even on melting it down and reshaping, the gold-content continues to exist undecaying. The gold, eternal though it is, has no eternal form of its own, apart from the transient forms given to it by goldsmiths. Thus, formless, it is invisible. Knowing the invisible gold-substance in one ornament means knowing the gold-substance in all gold ornaments. All the visible ornaments are real because of the invisible gold. Likewise with the world. All its visible forms are real because of the invisible Substance or the one undecaying Reality that pervades the whole of its being. Without the invisible gold the visible ornaments would be non-existent; without the invisible *ātman/ Brahman*, the goal of our search, the world would be non-existent. The pervasiveness of this Substance is not merely in the physical forms as in the case of ornaments. Both the physical and mental, both the object and subject, are pervaded by it, actualized by it. Knowing it as the substance of one's own being, all becomes known; knowing the one Reality, all becomes known.

Upaniṣads often opt to refer to the knower of this undecaying, all-pervading Reality as oneself, as a *dhīra*, literally, the one who knows and imparts his knowledge to others, used as a synonym for *jñānin* , the wise one. He sees one Reality in everything, flowing through everything (*paripaśyanti*). He perceives only the incessant flow of the creative self-expression of the one undecaying Reality in all the vagaries — often unpredictable — of life, whether in the day-to-day affairs of individuals and their problems, or in the unpredictability of life and the world in its entirety.

Any knowledge of the distinguishing features and characteristics of individual apparent forms will never be helpful in knowing the reality that appears as those forms. Not being the progeny of an ancestor, that Reality has no family line of its own; having no visible form of its own, It is invisible; having no differentiating features, to mind It is ungraspable; having no inborn character-colouring, It is colourless (*avarṇa*). It is limbless and has no sense-organs; It is thus sightless, hearingless, handless, feetless. All these showing what It is not, relevant when attempting to see It as distinguishable (*saviśeṣa*). Yet It is describable in certain other ways, as for example, the Eternal, the Omnipresent, the All-pervading, Exceedingly subtle, the Undecaying and so on and so forth, when intuitively perceived as having no specifying characteristics (*nirviśeṣa*). Yet the non-dual Reality being sought for is neither of these two; It is the ineffable experience in which both the *saviśeṣa* and *nirviśeṣa* aspects remain inseparably one, signified by the word *aksaram* (Imperishable) of the last verse.

Not intended for going into details of the teaching, this first section of the Upaniṣad merely clears the way for the real teaching that ensues.

It simply gives a glimpse of what follows in detail, giving an indication as to what the basic Reality to be revealed is, and what the benefit of attaining It would be.

यथोर्णनाभिः सृजते गृह्णते च यथा पृथिव्यामोषधयः सम्भवन्ति ।
यथा सतः पुरूषात् केशलोमानि तथाऽक्षरात् सम्भवतीह विश्वम् ।। ७।।

yathorṇanābhiḥ sṛjate gṛhṇate ca
yathā pṛthivyām oṣadhayaḥ saṁbhavanti ।
yathā sataḥ puruṣāt keśa-lomāni
tathā'kṣarāt saṁbhavatīha viśvam ।। 7 ।।

Spider emits out and absorbs back (its thread);
Herbs emerge out of the earth;
Hair grows out of the head and body of a living person;
Likewise too emerges this universe out of the
imperishable.

This verse throws light on how the Imperishable, the causal Reality, gives rise to the world from itself, with the aid of three analogies, in the same way that laboratory experiments are aids in modern science. The place of analogies in Vedāntic methodology is as decisive as laboratory experiments are in science. The value of experimentation in proving something in science is in no way superior to that of analogy Of this most scientists remain unaware. They, for example, in order to prove the universal fact that water is made up of oxygen and hydrogen, subject a drop of water to analysis. What is directly proved is that that particular drop of water is made up of hydrogen and oxygen. Taking it as an instance, it is extended to gain a universal dimension, and derived from this is the general concept that all the water in the entire world, even the water of the other worlds, if any, is made up of the same constituents. Likewise are all the other experiments. Vedānta's way of substantiating universal principles relying on analogies is therefore not only not unscientific, but is as scientific as any modern scientific method.

To verify the veracity of one scientific discovery by cross-checking it with further experiments is common among scientists. Vedānta too proceeds in similar fashion. When adopting more than one analogy to bring one basic principle to light, any detail not covered by an analogy is supported by another, three such being given here. The reality meant to be revealed so is to be intuitively visualized by putting all the three in the melting pot of contemplative thinking, not by taking each individually.

What stands out in the analogy of the spider is how the one Reality and the world are vertically related as cause and effect, how all the worlds emerge out of one substance and are reabsorbed into the same. That the spider brings out thread from its body and reabsorbs it has become a fixed imagery very dear to Indian poets, though the process, despite appearing so, is not a biological fact.

The analogy of the earth giving rise to vegetation, on the other hand, is more horizontalized in implication. Whilst effects arise from and exist not apart from the cause, all the multifarious facets of their appearance, such as existence, birth, growth, evolution, decaying and dissolution, along with the sowing of seeds for its cyclic continuance, are implicit in this analogy. That the effects, while not existing apart from the cause, have their own individuality and value at the transactional level, is also underscored by it.

The third analogy of the growth of hair on a living body stresses the indomitable, unsuppressible, unrestrainable creative life-urge the causal Reality has in it for emitting all effects out of itself—what Henri Bergson prefers to call *élan vital*, and Narayana Guru, *viśva vīrya* (the cosmic creative urge). The growth of hair on body is a sign of life; so too the emergence of all the living and inanimate beings as effects is a sign of life, signifying that the causal Reality is a living one. This inner urge for self-expression in the Imperishable Reality is called *karma* (action) in the *Bhagavad Gītā* (VIII.3) and it finds expression in and as all worldly manifestations, both horizontally and vertically. This inner urge in an active state is like a burning fire and in that sense is conceived as a *tapas* (a self-heating up process) in the next verse.

तपसा चीयते ब्रह्म ततोऽन्नमभिजायते ।
अन्नात् प्राणो मनः सत्यं लोकाः कर्मसु चामृतम् ॥ ८ ॥

tapasā cīyate brahma tato'nnam abhijāyate ।
annāt prāṇo manaḥ satyaṁ lokāḥ karmasu cāmṛtam ॥ 8 ॥

By *tapas*, *Brahman* swells up,
And thus is produced food;
And from food emerge
Prāṇa (life-breath), mind, the reals and the worlds
And even the attainment of immortality implicit in self-efforts.

How the causal Reality and the effect-world are related having been shown in the previous verse with the help of certain analogies, the present verse concentrates on the process of the emergence of many effects from one cause. What we are concerned with is a realm where no reasoning works, and so we need not expect that all the seers and sages would have the same visualization in their intuitive perception. Each *ṛṣi*'s vision is his own, incomparable with another's, yet all having a common frame of reference. For this reason, in each of the Upaniṣads we have a slightly different creation-picture from that in others. Still the concept that the causal Reality underwent a self-heating process called *tapas* is common to all, though stated in each Upaniṣad in a different way. For example, the *Aitareya Upaniṣad* says, "It looked intently at itself" (*sa īkṣata*) (II.i.1). "That which was self-born owing to *tapas*" (*yaḥ pūrvam tapaso jātam*) of the *Kaṭha Upaniṣad* (IV.6) and "He desired: let me become many. He underwant *tapas* with this desire." (*so'kāmyata bahuḥ syām prajāyeyeti, sa tapo'tapyata*) of the *Taittirīya Upaniṣad* are other examples.

Even physical raw materials must needs undergo some sort of heating up in order to get reshaped into a finished product. No factory works without using heat or energy. The creation of the world also involves a heating up process, though a subtle and all-pervading one, which will be more clearly stated in the next verse as taking place in and as the function of consciousness (*yasya jñānamayam tapaḥ*). Poets and artists too do their creative work while undergoing an intense self-heating process. A *ṛṣi* is also a poet or artist, the present *ṛṣi*-poet-artist being none other than *Brahman*. A human *ṛṣi* is an effect emerged out of this *Brahman-ṛṣi*. He perceives the same sort of *tapas* as the one undergone by that *ṛṣi* for bringing out of Himself the poem-like or art-like image of the world.

The order in which the creation took place is also conceived differently by different *ṛṣis*. The *ṛṣi* of the *Taittirīya Upaniṣad*, for instance, visualizes it as space emerging from the Self, air from space, fire from air, water from fire, earth from water, vegetation from the earth and human being from vegetation. In the present case, food is seen as that which first emerged from *Brahman*, followed by *prāṇa*, mind, the reals, the worlds, and finally the attainment of immortality implicit in self-efforts. The last stage, nothing other than the attainment of *Brahman,* completes the cycle. Such variations in the creation-pictures visualized by *ṛṣis* do not suggest that they were contentious on this point; it only shows that each *ṛṣi* had a mould of his own value notion in which he cast his creation story. The mould adopted by the present *ṛṣi* being a complex one, it demands a penetrating eye on our part to see the transparency of the picture.

While the 'food' of the picture presented in the *Taittirīya Upaniṣad* appears very near the fag end of the creation line, it appears as the first stage of creation in the present picture, showing how differently 'food' is conceived in these two contexts, the two belonging to different value systems. Food in the present context seems to represent the entire enjoyable world. How the creative urge (*prakṛti*) of the Self separates out itself into the enjoyer and the enjoyable world is portrayed by Narayana Guru in his *Ātmopadeśa-śatakam* thus:

> *Prakṛti*,separating itself out
> Appears as the enjoyer on the one hand,
> And on the other, it looms as everything external,
> Here as well as the hereafter,
> Referable as 'this',
> The expansiveness called the enjoyable world.
> (Verse 81)

These indications given by the Guru could easily be taken advantage of to meditatively perceive the creation picture represented here.

Food, the entity that first emerged from *Brahman*, is considered the source of all else. The rest of the items need not necessarily be taken as having emerged in the same sequential order as is suggested in the bracketing together of all those items in the present verse. This being only a preliminary chapter, and in view of the detailed creation picture to be discussed later under Section 1 of *Muṇḍaka* II, it would be out of place to discuss all the details of the creation story at this stage. Only a general picture, indicating certain cardinal points, is outlined in this chapter.

Nevertheless, leaving the phrase, *karmasu cāmṛtam,* freely rendered as 'even the attainment of immortality implicit in self-efforts', unexplained would not be justifiable. *Karma* (action) need not always be taken to mean the ritualistic actions of the Vedic context. All the actions we are engaged in our day-to-day life, all the physical, verbal and mental activities, are *karmas*. *Prakṛti* (nature) is always active. All actions are *prakṛti*'s. Even our thought about and search for Reality is part of nature's actions and thus are *karmas*. In the detailed picture of creation, to be portrayed in the second *Muṇḍaka* of this Upaniṣad, *karma* will be defined as *tapas*.

We the seekers are here as an effect of the *karma* or creative self-expression of *Brahman*; and in our turn we make efforts, or do *karma*, to trace back the source of ourselves in *Brahman*. This latter *karma* performed by individuals as part of nature's action is what we call *tapas* or austere self-discipline, resulting in the attainment of immortality and it is the *karma* referred to here as *karmasu-cāmṛtam*. The emergence of beings as a result of the *tapas* of *Brahman* and the individual beings' *tapas* leading them to realize the Immortal *Brahman* in themselves, together thus complete the life-cycle; *prāṇa*, mind, the reals, the worlds, all different cardinal apparent aspects in this cyclic process of emergence and re-emergence.

यः सर्वज्ञः सर्वविद् यस्य ज्ञानमयं तपः ।
तस्मादेतद् ब्रह्म नाम रूपमन्नं च जायते ।। ९ ।।

yaḥ sarvajñaḥ sarvavid yasya jñānamayaṁ tapaḥ A
tasmāt etad brahma nāma rūpam annaṁ ca jāyate ।। 9 ।।

All-knowledge, all-knowing,
Its *tapas* is act of knowing in essence;

Out of It emerge this *Brahman,*
Names, forms and food as well.

Calling the world that emerges from the imperishable Causal Reality (*Brahman*) also *Brahman* is profound in significance while being a poetically sweet image worth pondering on. The word *brahman* literally means that which unceasingly grows. The Causal Reality, being in the process of unceasingly unfolding itself, appears as the unceasing emergence or growth of the world; the effect-world also thus deserves to be called *Brahman.* Cause actually existing only in the form of effects, even as gold exists only in the visible forms of ornaments and the like, the effect-world is also as expansive as the Causal Reality. The expansiveness of *Brahman* and the expansiveness of the world are inseparably one.

The concept of the ever-expanding universe of modern science, of a universe that expands in all directions from every point of space-time, inconceivable though it is, could be thought of as akin to the 'this' *Brahman* that emerges from the Imperishable.

The self-swelling-up of *Brahman* caused by Its own *tapas*, pictured in the last verse, results in Its own appearing as 'this ' world, and thus It becomes 'this' *Brahman* (*etad brahma*), a concept in which the profundity and transparency of philosophical vision and the sublimity of poetical insight merge in the unity of the *ṛṣi's* intuitive perception. Perceiving cause and effect, *Brahman* and world, as inseparably one is the essential content of the Upaniṣadic vision. Signifying the two therefore by the same word — *Brahman* — renders the otherwise dry philosophical concept an ever sweet poetical image to be pondered upon.

Regarding the emergence of names, forms and food from 'this' *Brahman,* instead of taking it as having that sequential order, it could rather be understood in the sense that the effect-world is made up of names, forms and knowable/enjoyable objects. Narayana Guru's description of the world in his *Advaita-dīpikā* makes such a picture more transparent. He says:

Names in their thousands,
Concepts in their thousands,

And the ralated objects that loom in their thousands,
Together constitute the world.

(Verse 1)

The present 'this' *Brahman* is the aggregate world thus described, in which 'concepts' stand for the 'form' of the Upaniṣadic verse, every concept being a configuration formulated in the matrix of consciousness. Every such concept/form is denoted by a word, and both together represent an object known /enjoyed externally or internally. The world thus is not merely an external entity experienceable; it is a conglomeration of countless names, countless concepts/forms and countless corresponding foci of enjoyment into an ineffable experiential oneness. Such being the world, it has no existence apart from the Causal Reality, the Causal Consciousness, and thus the usage *etat brahma* (this *Brahman*) is highly suggestive in its significance.

The attributes *sarvajña* (all-knowledge) and *sarva-vit* (all-knowing) are also understandable in the same light. Consciousness in essence, as will become clearer as we proceed, *Brahman* is 'all-knowledge' as the original cause, and is all-knowing as related to all the effects that emerge out of, or get configurated in, It. It knows each and everything that emerges out of It. Both the attributes remain inseparable in the one Imperishable.

Khaṇḍa 2

With the transcendental knowledge and immanent knowledge having been distinguished in the first section, and an indication as to the theme of the transcendental wisdom given, the next section unravels how corrupt and vicious the immanent knowledge (*aparā-vidyā*) is, pertaining as it does to Vedic ritualism. Evidently it is aimed at creating an aversion towards it in the mind of the seeker, so that he would avoid promiscuous mixing up of the paths of rituals and wisdom. The seeker, released thus from the tangles of rituals and their worldly fruits, has to approach a Master properly to be instructed on wisdom, is stated at the end of this section.

तदेतत् सत्यं
मन्त्रेषु कर्माणि कवयो यान्यपश्यंस्तानि त्रेतायां बहुधा सन्ततानि ।

तान्याचरथ नियतं सत्यकामा एष वः पन्थाः सुकृतस्य लोके ॥ १॥

tad etat satyaṁ
mantreṣu karmāṇi kavayo yāny-
apaśyaṁs-tāni tretāyāṁ bahudhā santatāni ।
tāny ācaratha niyataṁ satyakāmā
eṣa vaḥ panthāḥ sukṛtasya loke ॥ 1 ॥

This is the truth:
Rituals the sagesconceived are variously elaborated on in the *mantra* part of the three Vedas. Perform them constantly, ye desire-mongers, thinking of this path to be to the world of merits.

The opening statement,"This is the truth", not merely concerning what is said in the present verse, is by way of an introduction to the whole of the section, meant to show the superior excellence of the path of wisdom over that of rituals. What is claimed here to be true is that superiority of wisdom. There are people with the fixed idea that what is meritorious in life is the performance of Vedic rituals meant for attaining the pleasures of heaven. Fully involved in and committed to rituals as they are, they would be willing neither to think of the world of wisdom nor to listen to wisdom teachings as of the present Upaniṣad. They will be unceasingly quoting from all the Vedas and the subsidiary scriptures justifying their perverse stand. The words of warning given here by the *ṛṣi* of the Upaniṣad are meant for the likes of them.

All the joys of this world are mixed with sufferings. What the ritualists consider attaining is painless pleasure, the highest good of life, available only in heaven. The door of this heaven would be open in the hereafter to those who strictly observe the rituals enjoined in the Vedas whilst living in this world. Such rituals in all their details are elaborated in the *mantra* part, the beginning, also known as the *saṁhitā* part, of the three Vedas, namely the *Ṛgveda*, the *Yajurveda* and the *Sāmaveda,* the other parts of the Vedas being *Brāhmaṇa*s, *Āraṇyaka*s and the *Upaniṣads*; this last one, forming the wisdom part, quite unheard of amongst ritualists. Such ritualists are here being forewarned by the *ṛṣi* of the Upaniṣad: "You ritualists, do stick on to your heaven-attaining rituals, but you don't see the trap you are caught in." The rest of the section discloses the nature of this hidden trap.

That the Vedas mentioned here are three in number whilst they were four including the *Atharvaveda* when the items under *aparā-vidyā*, were enumerated in the last section, deserves our attention. The *Atharvaveda*, not ritualistic as the other Vedas are, is of pre-Vedic origin according to historians. It is also the one Veda under which come the largest number of Upaniṣads. Excluding it from the context of ritualism is therefore understandable and justifiable.

यदा लेलायते ह्यर्चिः समिद्धे हव्यवाहने ।
तदाज्यभागावन्तरेणाहुतीः प्रतिपादयेत् श्रद्धया हुतम् ॥ २॥

yadā lelāyate hyarciḥ samiddhe havyavāhane ।
tadājyabhāgāvantareṇāhutīḥ pratipādayet
śradhayā hutam ॥ 2 ॥

Into the kindled fire,
At the very moment the flame blazes,
Should the oblations be offered with full faith,
At the very middle of the two halves of the melted butter.

To teach how burnt sacrifices are to be performed being not the objective of an Upaniṣad, which normally is that of the *Brāhmaṇa* portions of the Vedas, the present verse is meant to warn how inviolable and strict are the rules of rituals, though impracticable sometimes. Unless the oblations are offered strictly following the Vedic injunctions as to what oblations are to be offered, how offered, when to be offered, where to be offered, and the like, the intended result would not be attained. Some such sacrifices last for days together as is suggested by the plural word *āhutīḥ* (oblations). These oblations in certain sacrifices are first to be offered on either side of the flaming fire, intended as they are for the gods Fire and Soma, and then the main oblation is to be offered exactly at the middle of the two halves first offered. This middle point, in the jargon of ritualism, is known as *āvāpa-sthāna*. Non-compliance with such rules, even in minute details, renders the rituals fruitless according to the actual injunctions.

यस्याग्निहोत्रमदर्शमपौर्णमासमचातुर्मास्यमनाग्रयणमतिथिवर्जितं च ।

अहुतमवैश्वदेवमविधिना हुतमासप्तमांस्तस्य लोकान् हिनस्ति ॥ ३ ॥

yasya agnihotram adarśam apaurṇamāsam
acāturmāsyam anāgrayaṇam atithivarjitaṁ ca ।
ahutam avaiśvadevam avidhinā hutam
āsaptamāṁ stasya lokān hinasti ॥ 3 ॥

He whose *agnihotra* sacrifice is unaccompanied by *darśa* sacrifice (new moon sacrifice), the *paurṇamāsa* sacrifice (full moon sacrifice), the *cāturmāsya* sacrifice (four months' sacrifice), the *agrāyana* sacrifice (harvest sacrifice), without honouring guests, of unoffered oblations, without offerings to *viśvedevas* (all-gods), or of wrongly offered oblations, he thus destroys all his worlds up to the seventh.

The performance of large-scale sacrifices, some lasting for days together, is to be accompanied by various other subsidiary rites and vows. Not observing them in strict compliance with Vedic injunctions, would result not merely in the non-attainment of the desired goal, but would also bring about contrary results. As an instance of such Vedic constrictions details are given here of the subsidiaries that accompany the chief sacrifice called *Agnihotra*. The performance of *Agnihotra*, according to the Vedic injunctions, without strictly observing all the subsidiary rites and vows, would result in the destruction of all the seven worlds desired by the sacrificer. The seven worlds, as Śaṅkara suggests, could be understood in the mythological sense as the upper worlds of higher values called *Bhūloka, Bhuvar-loka, Svar-loka, Mahar-loka, Jana-loka, Tapo-loka* and *Satya-loka*, or else in a biological sense as the next seven generations.

Darśa is a sacrifice to be performed on new moon days and *paurṇamāsa* on full moon days. *Cāturmāsya*, as a sacrifice, is to be performed by householders once in four months — at the beginning of summer, the rainy season and winter — named separately as *Vaiśvadevam, Varuṇa-praghāsam* and *Śāka-medham*. The *cāturmāsya* observed by *saṁnyāsins* is of a different order. It is not a ritual. Wandering mendicants as they are, they find it practically impossible to move around in the four months of the rainy season. During that time they settle down in some place doing spiritual practices and teaching the locals. This they call *cāturmāsya*, literally the four months' vow.

Agrāyaṇa is a ritual performed twice a year, at harvest times, the newly-harvested grains being the main oblation offered therein. Only those who strictly perform all such sacrifices from time to time are competent to perform the main *Agnihotra* sacrifice. Performed otherwise, the results will be contrary to those desired.

काली कराली च मनोजवा च सुलोहिता या च सुधूम्रवर्णा ।
स्फुलिङ्गिनी विश्वरुची च देवी लेलायमाना इति सप्त जिह्वाः ॥ ४ ॥

kālī karālī ca manojavā ca
sulohitā yā ca sudhūmravarṇā ।
sphuliṅginī-viśvarucī ca devī
lelāyamānā iti sapta jihvāḥ ॥ 4 ॥

The Black (*kālī*), the Terrible (*karālī*),
The Mind-like-swift (*manojavā*)
The Brightly-red (*sulohitā*),
The Copper-brownish (*sudhūmra-varṇā*),
The Scintillating (*sphuliṅginī*),
The All-devouring (*viśvarucī*)
Are the seven flickering tongues of the (sacrificial) fire.

Fire is sometimes named *saptajihvā*, literally the seven-tongued. The seven tongues, each representing a different way the flaming fire appears, are enumerated in this verse. A sacrificer is bound to offer oblations to each of them individually.

एतेषु यश्चरते भ्राजमानेषु यथाकालं चाहुतयो ह्याददायन् ।
तं नयन्त्येताः सूर्यस्य रश्मयो यत्र देवानां पतिरेकोऽधिवासः ॥ ५ ॥

eteṣu yaścarate bhrājamāneṣu
yathākālaṁ cāhutayo hyādadāyan ।
taṁ nayantyetāḥ sūryasya raśmayo
yatra devānāṁ patireko'dhivāsaḥ ॥ 5 ॥

The one (sacrificer) who offers oblations
At the proper time whilst these tongues are ablaze,

Led by them (oblations),
Through sun-rays,
He reaches the abode of,
The one Lord of all gods.

This, along with the next verse, describes how a sacrificer, as he conceives and as taught in the Vedas, attains the goal he yearns for.

एह्येहीति तमाहुतयः सुवर्चसः सूर्यस्य रश्मिभिर्यजमानं वहन्ति ।
प्रियां वाचमभिवदन्त्योऽर्चयन्त्य एष वः पुण्यः सुकृतो ब्रह्मलोकः ॥ ६ ॥

ehy ehīti tam āhutayaḥ suvarcasaḥ
sūryasya raśmibhir yajamānaṁ vahanti ।
priyāṁ vācam abhivadantyo'rcayantya
eṣa vaḥ puṇyaḥ sukṛto brahma-lokaḥ ॥ 6 ॥

Saying to him "Come ! Come !"
The splendid oblations carry the sacrificer
Along the sun-rays,
Honouring him and saluting him with pleasing words:
"Here is the *Brahma*-world
Attained through your merits and good deeds."

प्लवा ह्येते अदृढा यज्ञरूपा अष्टादशोक्तमवरं येषु कर्म ।
एतच्छ्रेयो येऽभिनन्दन्ति मूढा जरामृत्युं ते पुनरेवापि यन्ति ॥ ७ ॥

plavā hyete adṛḍhā yajñarūpā
aṣṭādaśoktam avaraṁ yeṣu karma ।
etat śreyo ye'bhinandanti mūḍhā
jarāmṛtyuṁ te punarevāpi yanti ॥ 7 ॥

Unsafe boats, indeed, are these
Eighteen-fold sacrificial forms,
Said to be founded whereon are
Rituals the inferior.
Fools, esteeming it as leading to good,
Fall back into the very evils of
Old-age and death they intended to cross over.

Problemless, childhood is pleasant and joyful. Entering adulthood one begins to face the responsibilities, trials and tribulations that make of life an ocean of sorrows, also called the ocean of *saṁsāra* (*saṁsāra-sāgara*). One then feels the necessity to cross over this ocean; some try to find solace in drinking and the like, and a very few search for the meaning of life, if any at all.

The easiest and the most popular way of finding solace available to man is performing propitiatory and alleviatory rituals prescribed by priests and astrologers. Performing fire-sacrifices and *pūjā*s needs no effort, no understanding, no search, inviolable though their rules are. Observing those rules being the duty of the priest and not of the sacrificer, they do not worry the latter. Not a problem of his own interest, the priest does not care for those rules either.

Being so effortlessly available simply on spending money, most do not think of the stability of the boat they are on board. A weak vessel may get wrecked in mid-sea and the travellers may fall back into the very ocean that they wanted to cross over. This is the forewarning the *ṛṣi* of the Upaniṣad gives to those who board the boat of rituals to ford the ocean of *saṁsāra*, the ocean of births and deaths.

A definite and resolute end must needs have a definite and resolute means for its attainment, unlike a wobbling boat, that too too weak. The success of a burnt sacrifice, as is held by the Vedas, is founded on the stability of its eighteen factors — the sixteen priests, the sacrificer and his wife. The rules to be stringently followed in its performance, as the instances pointed out in the preceding verses show, are, practically seen, humanly impossible to comply with.

In the absence of certain items stated in the *mantra* recited as being offered, for example, betelnut, the priest appeases the sacrificer saying,"It doesn't matter; offering some rice instead would do." Any rule could thus be relaxed for convenience with the mutual consent of the priest and the sacrificer unmindful as they are of what it entails. To make the sacrificer satisfied somehow is the way of the priest, whilst the sacrificer's intention is to finish the ritual to the full satisfaction of the priest. Ignorant of the rules of sacrifices, a sacrificer could be appeased by anything a priest suggests, who on his part finds no difficulty in making alterations in the set rules. In actual practice, thus, sacrifices, strictly following Vedic instructions, are never performed.

Even if one manages to perform a ritual correctly despite all such snags, its results, the merits it acquires, are to be enjoyed in heaven only, and that too is unstable, the ritualist having to return to the earth and its sufferings once the merits get exhausted. Unstable indeed thus are rituals and their results, the boat ritualists board with the intention of crossing over the ocean of *saṁsāra*; in all possibility, instead of reaching the other shore, they fall back into the very same ocean. The *ṛṣi* of the Upaniṣad gives this forewarning to those who take to rituals.

As long as one thinks there is *karma* (action, ritualistic or otherwise) to be done, he feels himself to be its doer. He thinks, "I do this *karma*; its results too are mine", which binds him further to the bondage of actions instead of releasing him from it. All rituals performed with the goal of attaining final release (*mukti*) therefore only end up in making one more bound.

अविद्यायामन्तरे वर्तमानाः स्वयं धीराः पण्डितं मन्यमानाः ।
जङ्घन्यमानाः परियन्ति मूढा अन्धेनैव नीयमाना यथान्धाः ॥ ८ ॥

avidyāyām antare vartamānāḥ
svayaṁ dhīrāḥ paṇḍitaṁ manyamānāḥ ।
jaṅghanyamānāḥ pariyanti mūḍhā
andhenaiva nīyamānā yathāndhāḥ ॥ 8 ॥

Abiding in the midst of ignorance,
The self-styled wise, esteeming themselves as learned,
Do move around,
Trouble-inflicted-fools as they are,
Like blind men led by one who himself is blind.

अविद्यायां बहुधा वर्तमाना वयं कृतार्था इत्याभिमन्यन्ति बालाः ।
यत् कर्मिणो न प्रवेदयन्ति रागात् तेनातुराः क्षीणलोकाश्च्यवन्ते ॥ ९ ॥

avidyāyāṁ bahudhā vartamānā
vayaṁ kṛtārthā iti abhimanyanti bālāḥ ।
yat karmiṇo na pravedayanti rāgāt
ten'āturāḥ kṣīṇa-lokāś cyavante ॥ 9 ॥

Immature and variously living in ignorance,

They think of themselves, "we have accomplished, we
are content";
Ritualists' understanding, attached to pleasures as they are,
Is not proper;
Feeling afflicted and gained-worlds exhausted,
They sink down wretched.

Not mindful of the meaning of life, not knowing what one should gain by living, unaware of being immersed in ignorance, pleasure-mongers believe accumulating luxurious goods and consumables constitutes the meaning of life. Hedonism urges them on to perform rituals and charity deeds, hoping that such deeds will ensure happiness devoid of sufferings both here and in the hereafter, their guide in such matters being the self-styled-wise and the self-esteeming-learned. The performance of rituals as directed by such guides makes each of them feel, "I have made it."

This momentary sense of self-fulfilment vanishes in the face of new problems, quite normal in life as long as one views one's own life from perspectives motivated by personal interests and gains. Deluded are their minds by the longing for pleasures and pleasurable objects. They for this reason do not ever discriminate truth from falsehood, reality from appearance, the valuable from the valueless. They spend their life trapped in the vicious circle of rituals. Looking back at their own life finally, they perceive that whatever was thought to be making life meaningful has lost its meaning. They feel they have been wasting their life, with no more opportunity to make amends. What was expected of the next world, anticipated in value with the enjoyments of this world as criteria, would also seem a delusion on the loss of value of the joys of this world. Everything till then thought to be of great value here and in the hereafter thus appears useless and a sense of great loss and wretchedness fills their being.

The supposedly attainable heaven and its pleasures, if attained at all, are evanescent, as the next verse forewarns.

इष्टापूर्तं मन्यमाना वरिष्ठं नान्यच्छ्रेयो वेदयन्ते प्रमूढाः ।
नाकस्य पृष्ठे ते सुकृतेऽनुभूत्वा इमं लोकं हीनतरं वा विशन्ति ।। १० ।।

iṣṭāpūrtaṁ manyamānā variṣṭhaṁ
nānyat śreyo vedayante pramūḍhāḥ ।
nākasya pṛṣṭhe te sukṛte'nubhūtvā
imaṁ lokaṁ hīnataraṁ vā viśanti ॥ 10 ॥

Considering rituals and charity works as paramount,
The deluded are unaware of values still higher.
Having had enjoyment of the good results
Of their good deeds at the acme of heaven
They re-enter this world, or a still lower one.

Ignorance (*avidyā*) is the state in which one lives with the understanding that what is apparent, but in fact unreal, is the reality. Those who are used to living in darkness would be quite unable to think of life in the world of brightness. So too are those who live in the world of ignorance. They cannot imagine the world of wisdom and the nature of life therein, and are therefore called 'the deluded' (*pramūḍhāḥ*). Mind will be functioning in that world too, formulating sciences or scriptures (*śāstra*s) related to it. Such are the sciences or scriptures of rituals, founded not on reality and wisdom but on unreality and ignorance.

The merits, heaven and its pleasures, acquired through performing rituals called *iṣṭa-karma*s and through charity works, called *pūrta-karma*s, according to their own basic scriptures, are not for enjoyment for ever. The span of life in heaven is decided by the magnitude of the merits acquired while on earth. Such merits get depleted as one continues in heaven and finally when fully exhausted one is bound to come down and re-enter this world, to acquire more merits again.

Along with the idea that a world called heaven, wherein the fruits of one's good deeds are to be relished, exists comes the idea that an underworld, wherein one is bound to swallow the bitter fruits of one's evil deeds, is also there. Proving or disproving the existence of such worlds being not the objective of an Upaniṣad, the *ṛṣi* simply points out that both the worlds are meaningful only in the dark realm of ignorance. As the sun of wisdom shines, the darkness of ignorance is obliterated and along with it the worlds also.

'The other' (*anyat*) of the second line points to the way of wisdom, the really superior world, as is made more explicit in the next verse.

तपःश्रद्धे ये ह्युपवसन्त्यरण्ये शान्ता विद्वांसो भैक्षचर्यां चरन्तः ।
सूर्यद्वारेण ते विरजाः प्रयान्ति यत्रामृतः स पुरुषो ह्यव्ययात्मा ॥ ११ ॥

tapaḥsraddhe ye hyupavasanty araṇye
sāntā vidvāṁso bhaikṣacaryāṁ carantaḥ ।
sūryadvāreṇa te virajāḥ prayānti
yatrāmṛtaḥ sa puruṣo hyavyayātmā ॥ ॥ ॥

Undergoing *tapas* and full of faith,
Those who live in forests, tranquil in mind,
Erudite and living on alms,
Having no passions and attachments —
They attain through the door of the sun
The abode of Immortal *Puruṣa*, the undecaying *ātmā* (Self).

Contrary to the way of pleasure-mongers, the dispassionate way of renunciates is here made to stand out as an ideal pattern of life leading to its ultimate goal.

That the emergence of the world out of *Brahman* involves a self-heating process called *tapas* having been laid bare in Verse I.i.8, we return to the same *tapas* to be undergone by a seeker yearning to realize himself as *Brahman* in essence.

The seeker, the individual who has emerged out of *Brahman*, thus completes the cycle of *tapas*, resulting in his attaining his return to *Brahman*. Such is the nature and role of *tapas* as an austere self-discipline in the overall scheme of life's unfoldment. It presupposes a sort of agony and implies intensity of re-search, full of alertness, supported by a clear memory, willingness to give full attention to the problem at hand, and an open mind to listen and the will to believe, on the basis of correct scepticism that balances well with the will to believe.

Unrestrained wandering of senses and mind in search of gratifying objects renders life restless and aimless. Those who, with a clear notion of life's goal, restrain their functions in such a way as to be conducive to the attainment of the final objective, find themselves peaceful. This peacefulness is called *śānti* and those who live so are *śāntas*.

That there is a way of living aimed at an ultimate goal and what that goal is, are not known to most. The Immortal *puraṣa*, the undecaying Self, of the present verse denotes that goal, though, who or what that *Puruṣa* is and how to attain it would not at all be clear in the beginning to the one who intends to make life purposeful. Not knowing what it is, first he would have to believe in such a goal and in the possibility of attainning it, basing his search on the assurance of a genuine Master or on the words of assurance of former Masters recorded in source books or scriptures. This initial belief provides the beginner with a firm ground for his inquisitive self-effort through proper cogitation and meditative perception, which finally lead to his full conviction of the veracity of what he simply believed in the beginning. The initial hearing, or learning, of the words of instruction of a Master or scriptures with a believing mind is known as *śravaṇa*, further intense cogitation that ensues, *manana*, and the meditative inner search that eventually leads to the final conviction and intuitive perception, *nididhyāsana*. The initial belief in the words of one's own Master or of scriptures is known as *śraddhā*, translatable into English as 'belief', but quite different from the dogmatic belief in a theological sense. What is believed in *śraddhā* would no longer be a belief, once the final certitude is attained; but in its absence, with no firm basis to start from and a firm goal to be aimed at, no search and no attainment of goal would be possible. The initial belief it is that clears the path to the final conviction where nothing will be believed in any longer. Only on a goal fully believed in, our interest would unwaveringly be steadied.

Wandering mendicants as they are, *saṁnyāsin*s or the renunciates live on alms. What the generous and inquisitive people they encounter as they constantly move on, offer them is their only means of sustenance. Not at all considered respectable in a modern society though, this pattern of life of *saṁnyāsin*s has always been held in high esteem in India. *Saṁnyāsin*s on their part always make sure that they do not become a burden on anyone. Some of them, as Narayana Guru for example used to do, visit a home for food only after the dinner of the household is over, so that they can partake of the left-overs.

There is a tendency admittedly to treat those who live on alms as parasites of society, as they supposedly eat their bread without sweating their brows. *Saṁnyāsin*s do beg but not because they want to do. The values held high by them make them forget the need for toiling on the soil. Even in modern society, those who do white-collar jobs forgo the need for toiling. In the case of *saṁnyāsin*s, those who are benefitted by the high values they represent are always there willing to support them. It is thus a context in which society and *saṁnyāsin*s benefit mutually, with mutual support. Compared to the benefit society draws out of *saṁnyāsin*s, the worldly support they receive is negligible.

Attaining the Immortal *Puruṣa* 'through the door of the sun' is construed by Śaṅkara as the departed soul's reaching *Brahmaloka* through the bright path known as *archir mārga*, one of the two paths souls supposedly pass through on departing, the other path being that of *dhūma* or dark smoke. To accomodate such an interpretation 'the Immortal *Puruṣa*' of this verse is conceived by Śaṅkara as referring to *Hiraṇya Garbha* (the Golden Embryo), the primeval progenitor of the world as visualized by Vedic ritualists. The only word, if any, that is suggestive of such an interpretation is *prayānti*, translated often as 'depart' but strictly meaning only 'proceed on', suggesting the leaving of the world of rituals behind and proceeding on to the higher worlds of wisdom, as will more explicitly be stated in the next verse.

Given that this context is not that of dealing with the state of the departed souls but of comparing the values represented by Vedic rituals and Vedāntic wisdom, and that *tapas*, tranquillity of mind, erudition, and faith are considered essential prerequisites for the attainment of the Immortal *Puruṣa*, it seems bringing in the problem of the states of the departed souls would be far-fetched. Interpreting it, instead, as the attainment of Immortality of *Brahman*, the final goal of all Vedāntic enquiry, would be natural and understandable, which interpretation will also fit in with the claim made in the 13th verse to follow, that the ultimate goal of *Brahmavidyā* is the attainment of the Immortal *Puruṣa*. The sun could thus simply be taken as representing the Vedāntic way of wisdom as against the ritualists' path to reach heaven.

Given that the ritualists' attainment of their goal, the heaven, is through sun-rays, as was stated in Verses 5 and 6 above, and that the sun himself, not his rays, serves as the means of attainment in the path of wisdom, the sun-analogy becomes all the more meaningful. The sun and the sun-rays, conceivable as cause and effect, analogously suggest that what serves as the means to wisdom is the causal aspect of the effulgent Reality, and in the Vedic rituals it is the effect aspect. What leads one to visualize the Immortal *Puruṣa* is the search for the causal Reality behind all appearances. Nowhere in any of the Upaniṣads is it stated, or even suggested, that the Immortal *Puruṣa, Brahman,* is to be attained in a world hereafter. On the contrary is the oft-repeated emphasis that any meaningful attainment of *Brahman* is to take place here and now, for example in Verse 14 of the *Kena Upaniṣad*. This *Puruṣa* is none other than the live substance that abides (*śayati*) in the city (*pura*) of apparent forms constituting everything in all the worlds, from the most subtle animating principle in living beings to the ever expanding and never ending physical universe conceived by modern science.

Along with distinguishing the transcendental wisdom (*parā-vidyā*) from immanent knowledge (*aparā-vidyā*), this verse also points out who are the ones competent to attain the former. Such references scattered in various Upaniṣads were gathered by Śaṅkara and collated into a well-formulated scheme of discipline called *sādhana-catuṣṭaya-sampatti* (the four-fold prerequisites for attainment), which in the same form and sense was acceptable to Narayana Guru also, as is specifically stated at the beginning of his *Brahmavidyā-Pañcakam* (*Brahmavidyā* in Five Verses).*

परीक्ष्य लोकान् कर्मचितान् ब्राह्मणो निर्वेदमायान्नास्त्यकृतः कृतेन ।
तद्विज्ञानार्थं स गुरूमेवाभिगच्छेत् समित्पाणिः श्रोत्रियं ब्रह्मनिष्ठम् ।। १२ ।।

parīkṣya lokān karmacitān brāhmaṇo
nirvedam āyāt nāsti akṛtaḥ kṛtena ।
tadvijñānārthaṁ sa gurum evābhigacchet
samitpāṇiḥ śrotriyaṁ bramaniṣṭham ।। 12 ।।

Having well scrutinized the worlds build by rituals
A brāhmin should naturally grow indifferent to them;
The not-made is never attained through made-up means;
For the sake of attaining that (the not-made),
Let him go, fuel in hand, to a *guru*
Well learned in scriptures and well stabilized in *Brahman.*

---

* For details, see our commentary on that work.

The nature of *parā-vidyā* and *aparā-vidyā* having been laid bare, it is upto us seekers to choose one or the other. Rituals, their results repleting as they are, are to be practised constantly to ensure constant accrual of results. Exacting though their rules are, non-compliance with them will end up in unexpected, unfavourable results. Even their favourable results, though of heaven, are fleeting. The simplicity, sublimity and immortality of the results of *parā-vidyā* also having been discerned, any discriminating person will only grow indifferent to rituals and long for wisdom. Such are here directed, in order to attain their goal, to approach a *guru* well-versed in scriptures and well-stabilized in *Brahman*.

The one who thus happens to approach a *guru* is considered a brāhmin, the topmost of the four colour-grades (*varṇa*s) of human character according to traditional Indian psychology. Literally meaning the knower of *Brahman* though, here it stands for the one who knows that *Brahman* is the reality to be known ultimately, the one whose interest turns from the world of *aparā-vidyā* to that of *parā-vidyā*. In no way does it suggest at all that he is the one born of brāhmin parents. A brāhmin, as held by the *Bhagavad Gītā*, is the person whose interest is in acquiring wisdom and in passing it on to others, calmness, self-restraint, austerity (*tapas*), purity, forgiveness, straightforwardness and the will to believe being his distinguishing characteristics (XVIII.42). Such only discriminate between the two *vidyā*s and grow in longing for the wisdom of *parā-vidyā*; others, unaware of all such things, remain in the world of ignorance, taking the knowledge of that world as constituting *vidyā* or real knowledge. Brāhmin, as understood here, is the one who is aware of the darkness he is in and is desirous of getting out of it. The only person helpful in this matter is a *guru*, literally dispeller of darkness — *gu*, darkness and *ru*, dispelling. He is the enlightened person, one who knows what Reality is and finds himself one with it, as a wave that momentarily emerges out of the ocean of Reality.

Nirveda, known also as *vairāgya*, is the sense of detachment one feels towards sense-gratification and their objects. It also means distracting oneself from the ways of the Vedas, also hedonistic, their goal always pleasures of this world as well as of the other. Desire for pleasures dominates our life, according to traditional Indian psychology, when *rajo-guṇa*, the active modality of nature (*prakṛti*) prevails over us. Non-fulfilment of desires leads to feelings of wrath towards those who stood in the way, which eventually renders life hell-like. Desire and wrath (*kāma* and *krodha*) are always considered enemies by those who are on the path of wisdom (see *Bhagavad Gītā,* III.37). *Saṁnyāsins* (renunciates), for this reason, as part of their initiation ceremonies, undergo *viraja-homam,* a burnt sacrifice in which the entire *rajo-guṇas* and *rāgas* that go with them are symbolically burnt away at the altar of the Absolute, represented by the sacrificial fire, as was already indicated by the word *virajaḥ* in Verse 11 above.

The phrase *nāsti akr̥taḥ kr̥tena* is interpretable in two ways according to the order in which the constituent words are placed, which Sanskrit syntax allows in this context. Putting the words in the order '*kr̥tena akr̥taḥ na asti*', it means, attaining the not-made is never possible through any made-up means. The Reality we are in search of is the uncreated Immortal Substance, that is to say, It did not emerge as a result of any action. Attaining it also will never be the result of any action. That which is made of actions alone is attainble through action. No action or ritual, no *karma* of any kind, therefore avails in attaining the Imperishable *Puruṣa.*

Arranging the words of the phrase as '*akr̥taḥ na asti; kr̥tena kim?*' it would mean: "Nothing is here not made as results of action; why then yet another action?"

The entire cosmic system is in a state of constant change. Events occur in it every moment, everywhere. Every event occasions one state of existence of something to change into a new one. Transformation of one state of existence into another involves action, or rather that transformation itself is called action (*karma*). That which emerges as a result of *karma* is known as *kr̥ta.* There is nothing in this world which is not a *kr̥ta.* The actions (*karmas*) we willingly and deliberately perform also result in transformation of certain things already existing as the result of some previous *karma*. What action does is effecting such transformations; they never enable one to realize the substance that underlies all such transformations.

A *guru*, who intuitively perceives one Substance alone as existing, It alone as appearing here as himself, the knower, and as the entire visible world, the known, all together in a state of constant change, alone will be able to help a seeker attain his goal. No ritual avails there.

All the Upaniṣads, like the present one, are aimed at revealing the secret wisdom of *Brahmavidyā*, at revealing the Reality as well as is possible through the medium of words. Is it not then enough to learn such Upaniṣads carefully with full attention to reach the goal of attaining wisdom? Yet the very Upaniṣad tells us, one should approach a *guru*. Why?

Whether it is the secret wisdom of the Upaniṣads or any other subject of worldly interest, the knowledge we gain by learning by ourselves, reading books and through other means, depends on our method of approach, our grasping power, the conditionings and the resultant pre-conceptions of our mind, and so on. Not knowing what is deficient in our thinking nor what is wrong with our concepts and conclusions, each of us takes the way we resort to as the right one, and the ideas we formulate as the right ones, unless and until corrected by someone who is more enlightened. Any deficiency in our way of thinking, anything wrong in our basic notions, always distracts us from reaching Reality, so that what is unreal is mistaken for the real. Even the new ideas we gain thus and feel satisfied with could merely be the fantasies of an ignorant mind groping in the dark. *Jñānins* or *gurus*, the real visionaries of Reality, transparent in their awakened awareness, see how our thinking and understanding of the world are vitiated by such a basic deficiency, although we are completely oblivious of it. Fully enlightened of the Reality in themselves, they help others also to wake up to the Reality, nowhere else but in themselves. Only then can the others become aware of the darkness they were in till that moment. Until that moment each one wrongly believes that what he thinks, what he feels, what he understands, is real. While dreaming one thinks that all one encounters in the dream is real. Its unreality is realized only on waking up from the dream. So too, we live, we think, we formulate ideas and ideals in a dream-world. Its unreality will get revealed only on our waking up. This dream being a sustaining one, waking from it on one's own is almost impossible; a person already awake, a *guru*, is needed to wake us up. Reasoning or any other method, merely part of that dream, never helps us realize the unreality of the dream. All the efforts we make to gain knowledge through studying scriptures are simply part of the dream. Waking from this dream is what is understood by attaining wisdom.

That a seeker-disciple should approach a *guru* with a small bundle of fire-wood (*samit*) in hand is a traditionally accepted custom in India. Performing fire-sacrifice would be normal in a *gurukula* (literally, the family of the *guru,* the forest school where *guru* and disciples live together as a spiritual family). It symbolizes offering back to the totality of nature what is wrongly considered as one's own, one's possessions, motives, actions and even oneself, realizing that the individual has no existence or function apart from that of nature as a whole. Fire-wood, the most essential item in a fire-sacrifice, carried by a seeker, symbolically declares his willingness to dedicate and offer himself, like fuel offered into burnt sacrifice, for the cause of wisdom-seeking and also to be part of the fraternity. The fuel carried in hand also symbolically indicates what the intention of the newcomer to the *gurukula* is, making it unnecessary for the *guru* to make preliminary enquiries. Six seekers approach *guru* Pippalāda in the *Praśna Upaniṣad*, for example, also with fuel in hand, and the *guru*, on seeing them, asks them straightaway to stay with him a whole year, offering to teach them had they any question then, and if he knew the answer.

Who the competent seekers are having been mentioned in the last verse, the present one indicates who the real *guru*s are: they should be well-versed in scriptures (*śrotriya*) and well stabilized in *Brahman* (*Brahmaniṣṭha*).

Vedic literature collectively, consisting of the *Saṁhitā*s, *Brāhmaṇas*, *Āraṇyaka*s and Upaniṣads, is known as *śruti*, literally, that which is heard. The Upaniṣads alone being of wisdom import and the other three being related to rituals, a reference to *śruti* in any Upaniṣad points to only Upaniṣads in general with the *Bhagavad Gītā*, that condenses the essential teaching of all the Upaniṣads, also to be included, though it is traditionally considered a *smṛti* (literally, that which is remembered, the compendium of moral instructions codified recalling the basic teachings of *śruti*s).

One well-versed in *śruti*s is a *śrotriya*. In the sense that he has reached the farther shores of the teachings of *śruti*s he is sometimes called *śruti-pāram-gataḥ*. All the religious scriptures, in a broader sense, are *śruti*s and thus those who have assimilated the essential content of scriptural teachings are to be called *śrotriyas*.

We have just seen how scripture-learning alone does not make a *jñānin* of a man. A *jñānin* or *guru* is the enlightened person who has the experiential awareness of the truth taught in all the scriptures, and thus he has seen their farther shores. Reality being one alone, what all the *śrutis* try to expound and what the *jñānins* know are not two truths. For the same reason, no *guru*'s teaching can go against, or be negligent of, scriptural teachings. Spiritual teaching that respects no scriptures is therefore not worth considering sound and authentic. A *guru*, in this sense, is a person in whom the scriptural teachings and personal conviction coalesce into an experience of certitude and enlightenment, one validating the other.

Such a *jñānin* does not only know the Reality, *Brahman*, but he finds himself inseparably one with *Brahman*, as a wave is inseparably one with ocean, and thus well-stabilized in *Brahman*, he is a *Brahmaniṣṭha*.

तस्मै स विद्वानुपसन्नाय सम्यक् प्रशान्तचित्ताय शमान्विताय ।
येनाक्षरं पुरुषं वेद सत्यं प्रोवाच तां तत्त्वतो ब्रह्मविद्याम् ।। १३ ।।

tasmai sa vidvān upasannāya samyak
praśānta-cittāya śamānvitāya ।
yenākṣaraṁ puruṣam veda satyaṁ
provāca tāṁ tattvāto brahma-vidyām ।। 13 ।।

Unto one who has thus duly approached,
With thoughts tranquil and mind restrained,
Such an enlightened master teaches
Brahmavidyā down to its basics,
Whereby one gets enlightened to
Puruṣa the Imperishable Reality.

A properly qualified seeker approaching a proper *guru* sets the stage for the proper wisdom teaching to take place. The seeker's tranquil and restrained mind shows he is all prepared to throw himself into the situation.

Mind could get restless either due to stresses and strains in day-to-day life or due to an insatiable quest for knowing the real meaning of this riddle-like life. The former restlessness gets appeased by fostering a sense of detachment, and the latter by the belief and hope of getting the riddle solved through the wisdom about to be gained from *guru*. Either way, no restless mind will imbibe wisdom teaching.

A *guru* imparts his wisdom only to a disciple whose mind is all prepared to take it in. Each Master may adopt his own personal way of teaching yet the essential content of wisdom all teachers teach always remain unchanged. All teachings converge at one point in their basics. Ignoring these basics, common to all Masters, would therefore be not proper in any wisdom teaching. Any teaching based merely on the personal conviction of a teacher therefore would not be worthwhile. A teaching attains its finality and worthwhileness where all the basic principles and one's personal conviction and enlightenment find unity, one supporting the other.

All these particulars, the prerequisite qualities and disposition of a seeker, the qualities of a proper *guru*, how the scene is set for the imparting of wisdom, are detailed to us seekers as part of the teaching of Aṅgiras to Śaunaka.

MUṆḌAKA II

Khaṇḍa 1

DIFFERENTIATING *parā-vidyā* and *aparā-vidyā*, along with giving an indication of the glory of the Imperishable Reality the former reveals, was what was accomplished in the first section of the first chapter. How the *aparā-vidyā*, Vedic ritualism its most notable instance, traps one in a vicious circle, how one, on closely examining the two *vidyā*s and their benefits, grows reluctant to *aparā-vidyā* and yearns for *parā-vidyā*, which latter eventually leads him to the attainment of the Imperishable *Puruṣa*, and how a *guru*'s graceful guidance is needed in the final attainment, were delineated in the second section.

Now this second chapter (*Muṇḍaka*) depicts this Imperishable *Puruṣa*, the ultimate Reality, *Brahman*, as the causal Substance behind the emergence, sustenance and dissolution of everything apparent and distinct in this world.

तदेतत् सत्यं
यथा सुदीप्तात् पावकाद् विस्फुलिङ्गाः सहस्त्रशः प्रभवन्ते सरूपाः
तथाऽक्षराद् विविधाः सोम्य भावाः प्रजायन्ते तत्र चैवापि यन्ति ।। १ ।।

tadetat satyaṁ
yathā sudīptāt pāvakād visphuliṅgāḥ
sahasraśaḥ prabhavante sarūpāḥ ।
tathā'kṣarād vividhāḥ somya bhāvāḥ
prajāyante tatra caivāpi yanti ।। 1 ।।

That Reality is such:
As, from a well-blazing bonfire,
Sparks by the thousands issue forth, yet the same fire in essence,

So from the Imperishable, my dear,
Apparent forms many a kind emerge
And therin remerge too.

That what this Upaniṣad teaches is *Brahmavidyā* (the science of the Absolute) and that what this science reveals is the Imperishable *Puruṣa* have been made sufficiently clear in the first and the last verses of the beginning chapter.

The *Puruṣa* (literally, person) qualifiable as *akṣaram* is what we are concerned with now. The word *akṣaram* denotes the imperishable, the immovable, the constant, the immutable, considered here as *satyam*, a word translatable as truth, reality, honesty, moral integrity and so on. Here the word *satyam* stands for the crux of what is going to be taught, suggesting also that the Imperishable *Puruṣa* is none other than the all-pervading, all-sustaining Reality.

Satyam, as defined by Śaṅkara in his comments on the *Taittirīya Upaniṣad*, is: "Something, certain to be of certain form, and that form never altered, is *satyam*." The visible form and other perceptible qualities of everything apparent, we know, get altered. What then is of unalterable form is that alone which is formless! *Satyam* or Reality has therefore necessarily to be formless.

This *Puruṣa* need not necessarily be taken on a par with the *puruṣa* of the Sāṁkhya system where *prakṛti* (Nature) also is equally real. The *puruṣa* of the Sāṁkhyans is the changeless, witnessing consciousness in each of the living entities, and thus there are as many *puruṣa*s as there are living beings, whereas the present *Puruṣa* derives from the pre-Sāṁkhyan Vedic concept suggesting the one causal Being behind all the becoming, as, for example, conceived in the famous hymn known as *Puruṣa-Sūkta*. Neither is it a male as is likely to be misconstrued from the word's being of masculine gender. That the gender of a word is decided not by the sex of the object meant by it, is one of the peculiarities of the Sanskrit language. Each noun in it, is masculine, feminine or neuter in gender by its own right, regardless of its meaning. The word *vṛkṣa*, for example, though meaning tree, neuter in gender, is a masculine word. Certain nouns have usage in all the genders and certain others in two. The word *Puruṣa* though masculine in gender, therefore, need not be taken as denoting a male being. It simply connotes *Brahman,* the all-abiding, all-creating Substance, neither male nor female. Male and female principles both have their origin in fact in the one *Puruṣa,*the concept around which is built up the entire edifice of the teaching of this Upaniṣad. True to its etymological meaning — the one who dwells in the city (*pure śayati iti puruṣaḥ*) — *Puruṣa* is the imperishable Reality that abides in all that appears, even as gold abides in, and assumes, all the various forms of ornaments. The city the *Puruṣa* dwells in, individually viewed, is each apparent entity, organic or inorganic, that forms part of the world, and viewed universally, is the invulnerable cosmic system, while the individual and the universal are inseparably one, one meaningless without the other.

That from one Imperishable Reality, the *Puruṣa*, emerge all the apparent forms and all remerge back into the same, comparable to the appearance of sparks issuing from a bonfire, is the central idea of this verse as well as of Vedānta as a whole. Sparks in content are nothing but fire in essence, the minute carbon particle ignored by the *ṛṣi*s. So too the apparent forms that emerge from and remerge into the Imperishable Reality, in substance are nothing but that Reality. Though construable, when superficially viewed, that all beings in this world are born of one *Puruṣa* and they remerge into Him on death, this key verse warrants a penetrating insearch into its deeper significance so as to be true to the non-dualistic vision all the Upaniṣads expound and to be in line with the visions unravelled in the verses to follow.

The two key words of this verse that lead us to such a penetrating vision are *satyam* (Reality) and *bhāva* (apparent forms) which exactly in the same sense appear in the *Bhagavad Gītā* also in its Verse II.16. As was hinted at in our comments on Verse I. i.6 above, and as preferred by the *ṛṣi* of the *Chāndogya Upaniṣad, satyam, sat* in (*the Bhagavad Gītā*) could be understood as comparable to the gold-substance in all the apparent forms (*bhāva*s) of ornaments. All the ornaments emerge from one gold substance, remain as gold while appearing as ornaments, and continue to exist as gold when the ornament forms get destroyed. Gold, as substance, is formless and all the ornaments are forms assumed by it. Without gold the ornaments do not exist and non-existent gold cannot assume the form of ornaments. The ever-existing gold cannot remain without assuming some form, always transitory. What we perceive, in the form of a gold-ornament, is gold and ornament, the eternal substance and a transitory form, inseparably existing as one. Their separateness is a creation of our mind, an ideation; that is to say, our concepts. The two are separate in our mind, but in actual existence they are inseparable. Likewise is the inseparability or non-duality of the Imperishable Reality and the perishable apparent forms — the world. This oneness, this insparability, this non-duality, is perceptible only to the wisdom-eye (*jñāna-cakṣus*) of real philosophers, and only those of such a vision are to be called true philosophers. The *Gītā* puts it succinctly as follows:

> The unreal does not assume apparent forms,
> The real does not exist without assuming apparent forms either;
> What is hidden in between these two
> Is perceptible indeed to real philosophers alone.*

Such is the way the Upaniṣads and the *Bhagavad Gītā* visualize life. What we call birth is nothing but the transitory emergence of an apparent form in the already-existing imperishable Reality, analogous to the emergence of waves in the ocean, the sparks that issue forth from a bonfire, and the ornaments that get shaped in gold. Death, likewise, is nothing but the merging back of individuated apparent forms into the total Being, like the merging of waves into ocean and merging of ornaments into gold. Whatever be the form of ornaments that emerge and remerge, what exists indestructibly is gold alone. Whatever be the form of beings born and dead in the world, as the world, that which exists is always the Imperishable Reality alone.

The nine verses that form the rest of this section elucidate what is summarily stated in this first verse, going into the mysteriousness of the Imperishable *Puruṣa* as well as giving details of His emanations forming the world. This elucidation, besides, guides us in meditating on the *Puruṣa* as the original source of everything, including the one who meditates and his meditation.

दिव्यो ह्यमूर्तः पुरुषः सबाह्याभ्यन्तरो ह्यजः ।
अप्राणो ह्यमनाः शुभ्रो ह्यक्षरात् परतः परः ।। २ ।।

---

* *na asato vidyate bhavo na abhavo vidyate satah*
ubhayor api dṛṣṭo'ntas tv anayos tattva-darśibhiḥ
—*Bhagavad Gītā*, II.16

divyo hy amūrtaḥ puruṣaḥ sabāhyābhyantaro hy ajaḥ ।
aprāṇo hy amanāḥ śubhro hy akṣarāt parataḥ paraḥ ॥ 2 ॥

Effulgence in essence and abstract is that *Puruṣa*;
Existing internally and externally, He is the unborn;
Breathless and mindless, He is the Pure;
Even higher than the highest imperishable is He.

This Upaniṣad, as we have noticed, prefers to call the ultimate Reality *Puruṣa*, the city-dweller, also a synonym for *ātmā*, the Self. This city-dweller, this verse says, is effulgence in essence, as is denoted by the word *divyam*. Though usually translated as 'divine' with a religious leaning, the word, derived from the verb root *div*, meaning to be effulgent, really means that which is of the essence of effulgence.

The Self, the all-pervading Reality, is to be directly perceived by the seeker as the reality that pervades his own being, as Vedāntic methodology always maintains. The discrimination that whatever is 'mine' is not 'I' helps one directly perceive for oneself what the real 'I' is. Body, senses, mind, intellect and such other factors, usually taken to form 'my' being, are really 'mine' and that is why we say 'my body', 'my mind' and so on. Beyond whatever could be considered 'mine', what is found constituting my real being, the being that possesses all that is 'mine', is merely an awareness of beingness, pure effulgence in essence. Not merely the substance of my being alone, that effulgence is the substance of being in its entirety. The Imperishable *Puruṣa* is this effulgence in essence.

That the real inner content of anything is merely an experiential effulgence in essence is perceivable from yet another perspective. Normally we think of an object we perceive as existing externally. Let us examine the case, for example, of knowing a rose. Seeing it, immediately one recognizes it as a rose. The recognition, or rather re-cognition, is possible as the rose-idea is already in the mind. One who has never seen a rose in his life will not recognize a rose as rose. The re-cognition takes place as a result of projecting an already-existing mental image onto the object encountered by senses. Recognition thus is an event in which a mental and a visual image coalesce in one's awareness.

Still the object, rose, is out there, and its presence sensed. What our eyes sense are its form and colour; qualities of rose, not rose as such; what nose smells is its fragrance, another quality of rose, not rose as such; what is touched is its softness and tenderness, still qualities of rose and not rose as such. Whatever we perceive with our senses or imagine with our mind is one or another quality of rose and never rose as such, the qualified rose always remaining unperceived and imperceptible. The rose we supposedly see is only a functional mode of our consciousness. The real object, the qualified, thus exists really in our consciousness, as consciousness. So too when we say we perceive the world, what we perceive directly are its qualities alone, the qualified world always remaining unperceived. Its existence is in consciousness, as consciousness. And consciousness is pure effulgence in essence.

Amūrta is the Sanskrit equivalent to 'the abstract', its opposite *mūrta*, the concrete. The imperishability of reality (*satyam*) and the perishability of appearances (*bhāva*) were discriminated between in our comments on the last verse. That which has a distinct and definite apparent form alone is *mūrta*, a quality that goes only with transitory appearances (*bhāva*) and never with the eternal reality (*satyam*). The *Puruṣa*, in short, the reality behind the appearance of all concrete forms, is abstract (*amūrta*).

Births and deaths are relevant only in the realm of appearances. The emergence of a new form out of the already-existing reality is what we call birth, and the disappearance of an old form, death, even as the fashioning of a new ornament from already-existing gold marks the birth of the new ornament, but not of the gold substance. Likewise, the disappearance of an old form, on its being melted down, is the death of the old ornament, never of the gold substance. The substance remains always unborn. The *Puruṣa*, the Substance behind the appearance of all births and deaths, is similarly birthless (*ajaḥ*) and deathless too.

We think of the world we perceive as existing externally External to what? External to me who perceives. But am I not part of that external world? If so, I am inside the world, and the world is not external to me ! We are as if caught in a puzzle. It seems a puzzle only because the relative concepts of externality and internality are taken to be absolutely true. What appears relatively as inside and outside is the one absolute Reality alone, pure effulgence, or pure consciousness in essence. Externality and internality are really concepts or experiences that get shaped in consciousness. What is thought of as external and internal have their being only in consciousness, which in itself is neither internal nor external, or it is both internal and external simultaneously.

Prāṇa, literally, is the breathing function of all living organisms. That which survives through breathing is called *jīva* (*jīva prāṇane*), which word doesn't, strictly speaking, mean soul though often misconstrued thus. A living organism that can move around is often named *prāṇin* also. All such living organisms, along with their animating principle, emerge out of the one absolute Reality or *Puruṣa*. This *Puruṣa* is not sustained by breathing yet throbs from within with its indomitable and invincible creative urge for unfolding itself as everything, including all living beings and the animating principle in them. The original source of all that survives through *prāṇa*, while not itself surviving through *prāṇa*, is *aprāṇa* (breathless).

Man, of all living beings, with thinking for his distinguishing characteristic, is considered the most superior and is called *manuṣya* in Sanskrit, meaning the progeny of Manu, the originator of mankind according to Indian mythology, as is Adam in Christian theology, and literally meaning the thinking one. The emergence of mankind and his thinking, along with Manu, being from the Imperishable *Puruṣa*, that *Puruṣa* does not have thinking for Its differentiating characteristic, nor is It attainable by thinking, one of man's mental processes, being simply one of Its emanations. It is thus mindless (*amanaḥ*) in both these senses.

The connotation of *śubhram*, though translated as 'the pure', is suffusion of brightness, and therefore *Puruṣa* is *śubhram* in the same sense as It is *divyam*.

How one non-dual Reality could be conceptually differentiated as imperishable reality and transitory appearances, and how this differentiation, merely conceptual, does in no way affect the real oneness of what exists, we have already tried to clarify. It is comparable to the actual inseparability of gold and ornament in spite of conceiving the two differently, one indestructible and the other destructible. Given such a transparent vision of non-duality, how the non-dual transcendent *Puruṣa* is beyond even the imperishable *puruṣa* is understandable or rather meditatable. When the *Bhagavad Gītā* deals with this delicate problem, the conceivable twin aspects of *Puruṣa* are named *kṣara-puruṣa* and *akṣara-puruṣa* (the perishable person and the imperishable person) and the non-dual Transcendent *Puruṣa, Puruṣottama* (the most Supreme Person) (see XV.16-18). Such a portrayal of the *Puruṣa* in the *Gītā* could well be treated as an expansion of the vision signified by the phrase *akṣarāt parataḥ paraḥ* (even higher than the highest imperishable) of the present Upaniṣadic verse.

एतस्माज्जायते प्राणो मनः सर्वेन्द्रियाणि च ।
खं वायुर्ज्योतिरापः पृथिवी विश्वस्य धारिणी ॥ ३ ॥

etasmāt jāyate prāṇo manaḥ sarvendriyāṇi ca ।
khaṁ vāyur-jyotir-āpaḥ pṛthivī viśvasya dhāriṇī ॥ 3 ॥

From It is born breath,
Mind and all the senses,
Space, air, fire, water,
And earth, the all-supporting.

Prāṇa is the animating principle in living beings while *manas* is the thinking habit that distinguishes human beings. Both are phenomenal appearances that emanate from the one *Puruṣa* but, they are not the distinguishing characteristics of the same *Puruṣa*, inseparable from the *Puruṣa* though they are. Each of the numerous ornaments shaped out of gold has its own peculiarity, each serving a different purpose, yet remaining gold. *Puruṣa,* likewise, assuming the transitory phenomenal appearance of animating principle and thinking faculty still remains the immutable one. Animating principle (*prāṇa*) and thinking faculty (*manas*) are not the only phenomenal forms assumed by the *Puruṣa*. The less subtle and even gross phenomena such as sensations, sense-organs, sense objects, the aggregate of sense objects, the world, are all nothing but various manifest forms of the one *Puruṣa*. Intuitively perceiving one *Puruṣa* alone as Reality, therefore, implies perceiving the entire perceptual world, ranging from the most subtle animating principle upto the endless and ever-expanding physical universe, as not apart from that *Puruṣa*. Both reality and appearance are inseparably one, non-dual, even as gold and ornaments are inseparable. *Prāṇa* is the subtlest apparent form whereas earth (*pṛthvī*), representing all the physical worlds, is the grossest one, and in-between can be seen the entire range of phenomena, none excluded from the range of vision of this verse. Exactly the same is the vision enshrined in the following verse of the *Ātmopadeśa-śatakam* of Narayana Guru:

> Mental faculties, senses, physical body,
> Many worlds knowable contactingly,
> All are but divine apparent forms
> Of the one Sun that shines in the Transcendental sky,
> The one to be penetratingly searched for. (Verse 2)

The word *viśva*, though often understood as the Sanskrit equivalent of 'cosmos', literally means 'the all' — which sense alone holds good here. The earth is all-supporting in the popular sense that it supports all the constructions erected on it, all the trees and shrubs that grow in it, endures all the holes and tunnels made into it and everything done to it. Its all-supporting nature, more philosophically, could be understood in yet another sense according to Śaṅkara. The microcosm and macrocosm, the mental and physical aspects of existence, are basically constituted of the same substance, the reason why mental aspects are capable of grasping physical objects. The entire physical world, as conceived by Indian thinkers, is constituted of five basic elements: space, air, fire, water and earth; thuswise also are our five senses constituted.

The distinguishing feature of space (*ākāśa*) is its ability to transmit waves: those of sound, light and radio, all represented by sound. Ear, the sense-organ of sound, is in essence formed of the subtle aspects of space. The mutual interaction of ear and sound thus shows merely the essential oneness of ear and space. One's hearing a sound is thus really the event of forgoing the conditioning factors that differentiate ear and space and of realizing their essential oneness.

Air, the element one step grosser than space, has touch for its distinguishing characteristic, while possessing the quality of space:

sound. Skin, the organ that senses touch, is essentially air in content, and the event of sensing touch, is the actual event of realizing the oneness of air and the tactile sense-organ. Fire is the next grosser element in the line, which has, along with sound and the tactile quality, form for its distinguishing feature. Eye, the sense-organ that perceives form, is constituted of the subtle aspects of the fire principle. Water, still grosser in nature, has taste as its differentiating quality while having the qualities of the former three. Tongue, as the sense-organ for taste, is water in essence. Earth, the grossest of all the elements, has smell for its distinguishing feature while possessing all the qualities of the other four, and the olfactory organ is earth in essence. Earth is thus the one element that serves as the basis for all the other elements and in that sense too it is all-supporting (*viśvasya dhāriṇī*). Earth in the Sanskrit language also is called *dharā, dharitrī, dharaṇī*, all in the sence of 'all-supporting'.

The physical elements arranged in the periodic table of modern science are simply the sub-divisions of air, water and earth; the other two, space and fire, never counted as elements.

अग्निर्मूर्धा चक्षुषी चन्द्रसूर्यौ दिशः श्रोत्रे वाग् विवृताश्च वेदाः ।
वायुः प्राणो हृदयं विश्वमस्य पद्भ्यां पृथिवी ह्येष सर्वभूतान्तरात्मा ।। ४ ।।

agnir mūrdhā cakṣuṣī candrasūryau
diśaḥ śrotre vāg vivṛtāśca vedāḥ ।
vāyuḥ prāṇo hṛdayaṁ viśvam asya
padbhyāṁ pṛthivī hyeṣa sarvabhūtāntarātmā ।। 4 ।।

Fire is His crown point of head;
The sun and the moon form His eyes;
The directions of the compass His ears;
Multifarious knowledges His speech;
Air is His life-breath (*prāṇa*)
And 'the all' constitute his heart.
Out of His feet emerges the earth;
He indeed is the all-pervading substance (*ātman*)
Of all that has come into being (*bhūta*s).

The entire cosmos being the invisible *Brahman* visibly unfolded, visualizing it as the body of *Brahman* is a concept very dear to many of the Upaniṣads and the *Bhagavad Gītā*. This notional cosmic Person, in the *Brāhmaṇa* part of the Vedic literature, is known as *virāṭ puruṣa*, literally the person who reigns everywhere. The whole of Chapter XI of the *Bhagavad Gītā* could be considered as an elaboration of the vision condensed in the present verse.

Even as the modern concept of different worlds has in it the earth, the solar system, galaxies, nebulae and so on, so the ancient Indian concept of various worlds is that of the earth, the heaven, the middle-world, the under-world, sometimes the number going up to fourteen. The other worlds known to modern science are reachable by interstellar modules fired on to them, whereas the higher worlds of the ancient Vedic notion are attainable by fire-sacrifices offered devoutly by mankind to *deva*s, the inhabitants of heaven. The heaven in Vedism symbolically represents all the higher worlds. Reachable through fire-sacrifice, the crownpoint of the head of the cosmic person, representing heaven, is symbolized by fire in the present verse. Śaṅkara in his commentary also underscores fire as representing heaven. The *Chāndogya Upaniṣad* at one point also presents such an imagery. The two cosmic luminaries, the sun and the moon, that appear to be watching the world alternately by day and by night, stand for the two eyes of the cosmic person, another concept more popular among *ṛṣi*s as well as great poets.

Vedas, though customarily taken to mean the body of the four ancient scriptures of India, strictly speaking, means 'knowledge', speech symbolizing its articulated form. All knowledges, all sciences, are nothing but variously articulated forms of one consciousness, and thus expansion of the speech of the cosmic person. The emanation of the Vedas as the body of scriptures finds separate mention in Verse 6 that follows.

The statements, "The all (*viśva*, the cosmos) constitutes His heart" and "He indeed is the *ātmā* (the all-pervading substance) of all that has come into being ", put together, may look quite puzzling. The former suggests that all the worlds together form His heart, whereas the latter that every being has the cosmic person for its *ātmā*. But it would no longer be a puzzle if visualized with the help of the ornament analogy: all ornaments exist (potentially) in the heart of gold or rather as the heart of gold, and gold is the *ātmā*, the pervading substance, of all ornaments. *Ātmā*, though quite often misinterpreted as 'soul', in the Vedāntic context means the substance that pervades the being of something, the word deriving from the verb root *āt* meaning to pervade (*ād vyāpane*).

Everything emanating from the one cosmic person, the all-supporting earth derives from His feet, the all-supporting limb of body. So too air forms His life-breath (*prāṇa*).

तस्मादग्निः समिधो यस्य सूर्यः सोमात् पर्जन्य ओषधयः पृथिव्याम् ।
पुमान् रेतः सिञ्चति योषितायां बह्वीः प्रजाः पुरुषात् सम्प्रसूताः ।। ५ ।।

tasmād agniḥ samidho yasya sūryaḥ
somāt parjanya oṣadhayaḥ pṛthivyāṁ ।
pumān retaḥ siñcati yoṣitāyāṁ
bahvīḥ prajāḥ puruṣāt saṁprasūtāḥ ।। 5 ।।

From Him proceeds fire whose fuel is the sun;
From Soma, rain and herbs on the earth;
Males pour seeds in females,
Manifold creatures are thus born of the *Puruṣa*.

The only one source of all creations, the *Puruṣa* must needs be suffused with the creative urge for emanating everything out of Himself, and that urge must be active at every phase of the unfoldment of the cosmic system. Activating this urge, analogous to the activating of gods of heaven for worldly benefits through performing five-sacrifices, is counted as a *yajña*. How this creative urge finds expression in the actualization of virility, from the all-energizing sun to the actual implanting of seeds into the uterus of females, is treated as a sacrifice of five steps (*pañcāgni-vidyā*) here, following a similar but elaborate imagery depicted in the *Chāndogya Upaniṣad* in its Chapter V, Sections 4 to 8. Unless related to this *Chāndogya Upaniṣad* imagery, the present picture might appear to be lacking in cohesion. The *Chāndogya Upaniṣad* picture in its turn is a revised version of the Vedic concept of *pañcāgni-vidyā*, the five-fold ritualistic fire-sacrifice.

Vedism has it that man's happiness and prosperity in the world depend upon the fire-sacrifices (*yajña*s) he offers to the gods of heaven. A strict ritualist must, as Vedism enjoins, keep alive at home five sacrificial fires: *Dakṣiṇāgni, Gārhapatyāgni, Āhavanīyāgni, Sabhyāgni* and *Āvasadhyāgni.* This dependence of human life on *yajña* is given a revised and broader meaning in line with the Vedāntic perspective of life, as the dependence of all creation on the one creative urge of the one Reality that appears in different forms. As a result, a new concept of five-fold sacrifices finds its place in the *Chāndogya Upaniṣad.* We quote below the relevant passages, which follow exactly the same line of development of the creative vitality as is envisioned in the present verse:

> That world, O Gautama, verily is the sacrificial fire, the sun itself is the fuel, the rays the smoke, the day the flame, the moon the coals, the stars the sparks.
>
> In this fire the gods offer (the oblation of) faith. From this offering arises Soma (the moon), the King. The god of rain, O Gautama, verily is the sacrificial fire, the air itself is its fuel, the cloud is the smoke, the lightning is the flame, the thunder the coals, and the thunderings the sparks.
>
> In this fire the gods offer the libation of Soma the King. From this offering arises rain.
> The earth, verily, O Gautama, is the sacrificial fire; of this year is the fuel, space is the smoke, the night is the flame, the quarters the coals, the intermediate quarters the sparks.
>
> In this fire the gods offer the libation of rain. From this offering arises food.
>
> Man, verily, O Gautama, is the sacrificial fire; of this speech is fuel, breath the smoke, tongue the flame, eyes the coals and ears the sparks.

> In this fire the gods offer the oblatiton of food. From this offering arises semen.
>
> Women, verily, O Gautama, is the sacrificial fire; of this the sexual organ is the fuel, what invites is the smoke, the vulva is the flame, what is done inside is the coals, the pleasure the sparks.
>
> In this fire the gods offer the libation of semen. From this offering arises the foetus. (V. iv — viii)

That the offering of oblations at all levels is performed by gods (*devas*), representing the Reality effulgence is essence, and not by human beings, is to be noticed. It indicates that this *yajña* is one that takes place in the universal Existence. To treat the activating of the creative urge of *Brahman* as a *yajña* is a concept dear to the *Bhagavad Gītā* also, as when it says:

> The all-prevading *Brahman* is thus eternally well founded in *yajña*. (III.15)

तस्मादृचः साम यजूंषि दीक्षा यज्ञाश्च सर्वे क्रतवो दक्षिणाश्च ।
संवत्सरश्च यजमानश्च लोकाः सोमो यत्र पवते यत्र सूर्यः ॥ ६ ॥

tasmādṛcaḥ sāma yajūṁṣi dīkṣā
yajñāśca sarve kratavo dakṣiṇāśca ।
saṁvatsaraśca yajamānaśca lokāḥ
somo yatra pavate yatra sūryaḥ ॥ 6 ॥

The *yajus* formulas, the initiation rites,
And all the *yajña*s, all the *kratu*s and all sacrifical gifts,
The year, the sacrificer too, and the worlds attainable
Wherein purifyingly shines the moon and the sun too;

That all the factors that upkeep the cosmic order and sustain life emerge from one cosmic person as *yajña*s, having been shown in the last verse, now the actual *yajña*s, the rituals enjoined the Vedas, themselves are conceived as originating from the same *Puruṣa*. Properly performed *yajñas* involve numerous factors, though not all are mentioned here, and they are all supposed to have emanated from the one *Puruṣa*. What is important to note is the comprehensiveness of the context under consideration and not the exact number of items actually mentioned.

The *yajña* conceived in the last verse ensured the upkeep of the cosmic order and life, all as spontaneous self-unfoldment of the one *Puruṣa*. The Vedic *yajñas*, the actual rituals, on the other hand, were conceived by human mind under the compulsion of certain convictions and value notions. Man, his mind, his convictions, his value notions, all being nothing but constituent elements of the cosmic system, these *yajnas* are not to be simply ignored as superstitious fantasies or religious expressions of the people of a primitive culture.

Each verse of the *Ṛgveda*, the most ancient and original of all the Vedas, is known as a *ṛk*; and each verse of the *Sāmaveda*, a musical re-rendition of certain parts of the *Ṛgveda*, intended for chanting at rituals, is known as a *sāma*; and *Yajurveda* is yet another re-rendition of parts of the *Ṛgveda* meant for actual performance of rituals, and each of its stanzas is known as a *yajus*.

Dīkṣā is the initiation the sacrificer (*yajamāna*) and the priests have to undergo before the beginning of a ritual. Sacrifices, according to their nature, are sometimes classified as *yajñas* and *kratus*, the former involving no animal sacrifice, the latter involving it. *Dakṣiṇā* encompasses the gifts to be offered to the priests at the successful completion of a ritual. Literally meaning 'year', the word *samvatsara* refers to the appropriate auspicious time of the year fixed for the conducting of a sacrifice. *Yajamāna* is the sacrificer for whose sake the sacrifice is performed and who finances it. *Lokāḥ* (worlds) indicates the worlds attainable as the end result of performing the ritual. Certain souls, as conceived by ritualists, reach the world of the moon through the dark path of smoke (*candra-loka*) to return to this world again as the merits acquired deplete. Certain other souls, via the path of bright flames, reach the world of the sun (*sūrya-loka*), never to return.

तस्माच्च देवा बहुधा सम्प्रसूताः साध्या मनुष्याः पशवो वयांसि ।
प्राणापानौ व्रीहियवौ तपश्च श्रद्धा सत्यं ब्रह्मचर्यं विधिश्च ।। ७ ।।

tasmācca devā bahudhā samprasūtāḥ
sādhyā manuṣyāḥ paśavo vayāmsi ।
prāṇāpānau vrīhiyavau tapaśca
śraddhā satyaṁ bramacaryaṁ vidhiśca ॥ 7 ॥

From Him are manifoldly born,
Gods, *sādhya*s, men, cattle, birds,
In-breath and out-breath, rice and barley,
Austerity, faith, truth, *brahmacarya* and moral codes.

Going into further details of the emanations of the one *Puruṣa*, this verse points to beings and entities belonging to various levels of existence and various worlds of interest. First it mentions various beings of various worlds, then the vital life-function represented by *prāṇa* (in-breath) and *apāna* (out-breath) in all of them, then food that nourishes all, and finally different aspects of spiritual discipline a seeker undergoes in order to attain the *Puruṣa* as the reality in oneself, all emanating from the one *Puruṣa*.

Many are the worlds conceived by Indian poets and seers: sometimes three in number and sometimes even fourteen — seven above the earth and seven below excluding the earth. Each world is conceived as dominated by a different kind of living beings, as man dominates the life on earth. Whether such worlds and their inhabitants really do exist is not considered to be a serious problem. Even in this world beings are categorized as belonging to the kingdoms of minerals, vegetables and animals, man placed at the topmost rung of the last one. The nature of existence of vegetables would naturally be quite incomprehensible to minerals, if they do have mind. The nature of animal life would likewise be incomprehensible to vegetables. So too is human life and its mobility and achievements to other animals. The life above the human world, if any, would likewise be incomprehensible to the human mind. The inadequacy of human mind to comprehend something should never be considered the criterion for deciding whether those things exist or do not. The seers of India, therefore, instead of conclusively saying that no such worlds exist, in their poetically rich mind, thought of many imaginary worlds and their inhabitants like *deva*s, *gandharva*s, *kinnara*s, *sādhya*s and so on. Likewise with the imaginary lower worlds. Whatever be the worlds, whatever the beings inhabiting them, all of them have only one original source — the one *Puruṣa*. Given that all the worlds, including this one, do have existence only as emanations imagined by the one and only *Puruṣa*, the sharpness of the question as to whether such worlds and beings do exist or not, also gets blunted.

Perceiving the one *Puruṣa* alone in everything and also viewing one's own life accordingly, is a rare occurrence in the normal course of human life. Mankind is more interested in worldly affairs and the pleasures they offer. Their attention rarely turns to the Reality, sure as they are of the prospect of having the more and more pleasures by making more and more efforts and unheard of the eternal joy of attaining immortality just by knowing the Reality, the undecaying *Puruṣa* in oneself. The seekers of the Reality subject themselves to a certain self-discipline as a means to their final goal, even as the worldly-minded pursue worldly means to attain their worldly gains. Such disciplines are represented here by *tapas* (austerity or self-heating-up), *śraddhā* (faith), *satyam* (truth and honesty), *brahmacarya* (treading the path of *Brahman* in life or transforming one's own life into a search for *Brahman*) and *vidhi* (abiding by moral codes). The implications of the first two were discussed in detail in our comments on Verse I.ii.11, and *brahmacarya* and *satya* will be dealt with in detail later under Verse III.i.5. *Vidhi* implies to comply with moral injunctions enjoined either by scriptures or with state-made laws. More important than such compliances is the compliance with the moral compulsion from within oneself as one becomes aware of one's own place and role in the overall scheme of life.

Even such means of attaining the *Puruṣa* have their source in the very same *Puruṣa*.

सप्त प्राणाः प्रभवन्ति तस्मात् सप्तार्चिषः समिधः सप्त होमाः ।
सप्त इमे लोका येषु चरन्ति प्राणा गुहाशया निहिताः सप्त सप्त ॥ ८ ॥

sapta prāṇāḥ prabhavanti tasmāt
saptārciṣaḥ samidhaḥ sapta homāḥ ।
sapta ime lokā yeṣu caranti prāṇā
guhāśayā nihitāḥ sapta sapta ॥ 8 ॥

From Him come forth the seven *prāṇa*s,
The seven flames, their seven fuels, the seven oblations,
These seven worlds wherein move the *prāṇa*s,
Inhabiting a secret abode of a seven-in-seven system.

Seven *prāṇa*s and their functions are what are visualized in this verse as emerging from the one *Puruṣa*. The *prāṇa*s' function being seven-fold at all stages shows how that which comes forth from the *Puruṣa* is all well-structured and coherent. The well-known *prāṇa*s of Vedāntic literature are not seven, but five in number — *prāṇa*, *apāna, vyāna, udāna, samāna* — whose functions are well related in the second section of the *Praśna Upaniṣad*. No reference to the number of *prāṇas* as seven is to be found in any other Upaniṣad or other basic scriptures. The present seven *prāṇa*s could better be understood as allegorically referring to some vital function other than those related to life-breath. The seven, as Śaṅkara proposes, represent the seven bodily orifices: two eyes, two ears, two nostrils and the mouth. Whereas Narayana Guru in his *Homa Mantram* (sacred formula for burnt sacrifice), allegorically conceives the five senses, mind and intellect as seven flames of the fire of consciousness, into which are offered their respective objects as oblation, the result, the apparent blazing up of the one consciousness in seven forms of perceptual knowledge, similar to the blazing up of seven flames out of the same fire. The original *mantra* of the Guru is as follows:

oṁ agne tava yat tejas tad brāhmam
atas tvam pratyakṣam brahmāsi
tvadīyā indriyāṇi mano-buddhir-iti sapta-jihvāḥ
tvayi viṣayā iti samidho juhomi
aham ity ājyam juhomi
tvam naḥ prasīda prasīda
śreyaśca preyaśca prayaccha svāhā !
oṁ śāntiḥ śāntiḥ śāntiḥ.

Translated, it reads:

O Fire, thy effulgence is that of *Brahman;*
Thou, therefore, art *Brahman* become perceptible;
Unto thee, having five senses,

mind and intellect for seven tongues.
I offer as oblations their respective objects;
I then offer unto thee clarified butter
Representing my 'I-sense' ;
Be pleased with us! May thou be pleased!
May thou be pleased to bestow on us
The worldly values as well as the higher values.
svāhā !
Oṁ Peace ! Peace ! Peace !

The similarity of the imagery in this *mantra* with that of the present verse of the Upaniṣad is striking and unparalleled. It was perhaps inspired by this Upaniṣadic verse that the Guru conceived the idea of this particular symbolic fire sacrifice.

The present Upaniṣad in its Verse I.ii.4 has named the seven flames of fire as Kālī, Karālī, Manojavā, Sulohitā, Sudhūmravarṇā, Sphuliṅginī, and Viśvarucī. The present seven-fold offerings also could well be conceived as entailing that seven-flamed-fire concept.

The five senses, mind and intellect are the outlets for consciousness to express itself functionally and are also the inlets for objects to enter and enliven consciousness. Their functional liveliness is conceived here as their flames (*arciṣ*). The object each sense comes in contact with in each instance, that makes consciousness blaze, is the fuel (*samit*) and the event of sense contact is the act of offering (*homam*). The resultant sense experience and the accompanying pleasures and pains constitute the worlds attained (*lokāḥ*). The moving around of the senses is always in the world of such experiences (*yeṣu caranti prāṇāḥ*).

Senses, being not merely the physical organs such as ears and eyes, are subtle in essence. Their existence and function, therefore, are considered here as inhabiting a secret abode (*guha*). The neo-classic Vedānta considers this realm as *sūkṣma śarīra* (the subtle body), though this is a notion not known either to the Upaniṣads or the *Bhagavad Gītā*.

अतः समुद्रा गिरयश्च सर्वेऽस्मात् स्यन्दन्ते सिन्धवः सर्वरूपाः ।
अतश्च सर्वा ओषधयो रसश्च येनैष भूतैस्तिष्ठते ह्यन्तरात्मा ।। ९ ।।

ataḥ samudrā girayaśca sarve
asmāt syandante sindhavaḥ sarvarūpāḥ ।
ataśca sarvā oṣadhayo rasaśca
yenaiṣa bhūtaistiṣṭhate hyantarātmā ॥ 9 ॥

From Him arise all the seas and mountains,
From Him roll out rivers of every kind;
And from Him all herbs, their sap
Whereby is upheld the interior self (the *Puruṣa*)
Along with His manifest forms.

Topography of land, its topmost level the mountains and the lowest level the seas, with land and life in-between, is what is seen in this verse as originating from the *Puruṣa*. The sap (*rasa*) of vegetables not only forms their sap of life, but it also sustains animal life on land, interlinking all varieties of living beings as belonging to an overall ecological system. The existence of one type of being ensures the happiness or existence of some other beings in that life-system. Experiencing joy, another denotation of the word *rasa*, thus is also integrally related to the sap (*rasa*) of herbs and vegetables. This *rasa* (sap) that emerges from the one *Puruṣa*, through its capacity to sustain the overall eco-system, each living being ensuring the *rasa* (joy) of others, thuswise supports all *bhūta*s (everything that has come into being), the manifest forms of the same *Puruṣa*. The *antarātmā* (interior self) of this verse is none other than the *Puruṣa* in His capacity as the substance that pervades all that has emerged from Himself.

पुरूष एवेदं विश्वं कर्म तपो ब्रह्म परामृतम्।
एतद् यो वेद निहितं गुहायां सोऽविद्याग्रन्थिं विकिरतीह सोम्य ॥ १० ॥

puruṣa evedaṁ viśvaṁ
karma tapo brahma parāmṛtam ।
etad yo veda nihitaṁ guhāyāṁ
so'vidyā-granthiṁ vikiratīha somya ॥ 10 ॥

Puruṣa indeed is all this —
(Vedic) rituals, (Vedāntic) austere self-enquiry,
The transcendental and immortal *Brahman*.

He who knows Him as abiding in their secret abode,
He, here on earth, my dear, rends asunder the knots of ignorance.

That everything in all the worlds is only one *Puruṣa* in essence and is the manifest form in which He expresses Himself, is the one point emphasized all through this section and recapitulated in this concluding verse. Knowing one *Puruṣa* is therefore knowing everything in all the worlds, the point that takes us back to the original question with which this Upaniṣad began: Knowing what will all this world becomes known? The answer is: Knowing the one *Puruṣa* all the worlds become known.

The followers of Vedism resort to rituals (*karmas*) and of Vedāntism to austere self-enquiry (*tapas*) as ways to attain their respective goals, heaven for the former and final release (*mukti*) for the latter. Both methods are nothing but two ways in which the *Puruṣa*-reality in the seeker finds self-expression. What differentiates the two kinds of seekers is simply that the former are ignorant of this reality while the latter are aware of it and thus not bound to any *karma*s (actions, rituals). Ignorant as they are of the reality that all *karma*s (actions) are of the one *Puruṣa*, not of individuals, ritualists make the mistake of regarding the *karma*s as their's and become much attached to their aimed-at-goal, a vicious circle in effect, here called *avidyā-granthi* (the knot of ignorance), the details of which were discussed in Section 2 of the first *Muṇḍaka*. Those alone who are aware of the one *Puruṣa* cut asunder this knot and come out of the vicious circle, which attainment is nothing other than the Final Release, *mukti* or *mokṣa*.

The final Release, unlike what is conceived by ritualists in their ignorance, is to be attained here in this world. As that which we consider to be the other world is not outside the one *Puruṣa*, the knower of that *Puruṣa* transcends the difference between the here and the hereafter. Our concern for *mukti* being while living in this world, its attainment also would be of value only in this world, a point underscored in the last line of this verse which says: "here on earth" (*iha*).

Still it seems as if the *Puruṣa* is hiding in a cave. How to attain Him is the theme of the next section.

Khaṇḍa 2

आविः सन्निहितं गुहाचरं नाम महत् पदमत्रैतत् समर्पितम् ।
एजत् प्राणन्निमिषच्च यदेतज्जानथ सदसद्वरेण्यं परं
विज्ञानाद् यद्वरिष्ठं प्रजानाम् ।। १।।

āviḥ sannihitaṁ guhācaraṁ nāma
mahat padam atraitat samarpitam ।
ejat prāṇannimiṣacca yadetaj
jānatha sadasad-vareṇyaṁ paraṁ
vijñānād yadvariṣṭhaṁ prajānām ।। 1 ।।

Intimately manifest and well-known as moving-in-secret
Is the great goal attainable.
In it reposes all that moves, breathes and blinks;
Know It as reality as well as appearence.
The best of all desirables for all,
The transcendental, beyond man's all specific knowledge.

Parā-vidyā and *aparā-vidyā* having been discriminated between, the captivating yet ensnaring nature of the latter *vidyā* detailed, and the one *Puruṣa*, out of whom everything emerges and knowing whom all the worlds become known, delineated, we now move on to see how this one *Puruṣa* is to be sought and the nature of the certitude such a search brings about.

That the *Puruṣa* is the most intimate of all realities and that It is effulgence in essence are both connoted by the word *āviḥ* (intimate). Whether something is near or not is decided with one's own being as basis. For each one, the nearest of all entities is one's own being, which is itself pure consciousness or effulgence in essence, as was seen in Verse 2 of the last section. The most easily accessible and undeniable reality being one's own self-content, itself being nothing but a sparking of the great bonfire of the one Reality, the easiest way to seek the *Puruṣa* is in the search for one's own self-content.

Guhā-caram, though literally meaning 'moving inside a cave', is rendered here as 'moving-in-secret', to be true to the Vedāntic speculation in general, more metaphysical than theological in nature.

The theological concept of soul it is that lured certain interpreters to conceive that the *Puruṣa* is seated in the heart's cave, in spite of all that was stated to the contrary in the last section. The cave (*guha*) could better be allegorically understood as representing the *Puruṣa's* invisibility and indistinctness. What is distinct and visible is always an apparent form, and not the substance underlying it. The *Puruṣa* as such, being the substance that underlies all apparent forms in all the worlds, is formless and therefore invisible yet indubitably existing. It is as though its existence is in darkness like within a cave. The means we choose to attain such a *Puruṣa* must needs be a fitting one.

Mahat-padam is translated as 'the great goal attainable', *mahat* meaning 'the great' and *padam*, goal. *Mahat* is a word with a vast range of meanings such as extensiveness, superiority, richness, prowess, lasting nature and the like, all relevant to *Brahman*, the *Puruṣa*. *Padam* also means 'the word', here referring to *AUṀ*, the one-syllabled word that represents the Absolute, the *Puruṣa*. The means chosen should befit such a goal.

To move, to breathe, to blink are signs of life, all in accordance with *Puruṣa*, a living Reality, or rather the only living Reality. All living entities in all the worlds are mere transitory sparks from that eternally living Reality and as such all of them repose within It. The seeker, now aiming at that Reality, is but one of the countless sparks of this one Reality. In him (the seeker) too are visible all the signs of life. What he intends to attain is the Reality he emanated from, which he is inseparable from. Perceiving that Reality as an external object is therefore out of question. That the means chosen should befit this Reality is underscored by the phrase *etat jānatha* (know It).

A further guideline for choosing the proper method of enquiry is stated: It is reality as well as appearance at the same time. How substance alone is real and appearance is unreal we have discussed in detail with the analogy of gold and ornaments. As ornaments and gold are mutually inseparable so *Puruṣa* and all the worlds are inseparably one. Such is the reality the seeker is in search of and the means chosen by him should match the goal sought.

The reality most easily attainable to anyone is that within oneself, which is a spark of *Puruṣa*. Knowing it becomes knowing the *Puruṣa*, the best of all desirables, the awareness indeed that cuts asuder all the knots of ignorance.

Any knowledge one gains of an object would be a specific one; the knowledge of the one reality underlying all the objects in all worlds, being the reality underlying the seeker also, however cannot be made an object of knowledge, and the real knowledge of that reality will not be specific either. A non-objective knowledge of the reality is beyond man's all specific types of knowledge, as it is a knowledge even above all knowledge, as Narayana Guru would prefer to put it. Such is the Reality and Knowledge we are now seeking a means to attain.

यदर्चिमद् यदणुभ्योऽणु च यस्मिंल्लोका निहिता लोकिनश्च ।
तदेतदक्षरं ब्रह्म स प्राणस्तदु वाङ् मनः तदेतत् सत्यं तदमृतं तद् वेद्धव्यं सोम्य
विद्धि ॥ २ ॥

yad arcimad yad aṇubhyo'ṇu ca
yasmin lokā nihitā lokinaś ca ।
tad etad akṣaraṁ brahma sa prāṇas tadu vāṅ manaḥ
tad etad satyaṁ tad amṛtaṁ tad veddhavyaṁ somya
viddhi ॥ 2 ॥

Spontaneously ablaze, subtler than the subtle is It;
In It are set all the observable worlds and their observers;
It is the Imperishable *Brahman*;
It appears as *prāṇa*; It appears as speech and mind;
It is the Real; It is the Immortal;
That is the target (that is to be known);
My dear, do aim at That (do know That).

Now that the *Puruṣa* as pure unconditioned consciousness in essence has been revealed in our comments on Verse II.i.2, and how that unconditioned consciousness blazes assuming conditioned manifest forms of various kinds of perceptions has been clearly seen in Verse II.ii.8, how it is spontaneously ablaze should be quite clear to penetrating minds. By this blazing of pure consciousness conditioned forms of appearance are assumed, urged on by the invincible creative drive from within Itself, which urge in Vedānta is known as *karma* (action), as is made sufficiently clear in Verse VIII.3 of the *Bhagavad Gītā,* where it says;

> That creative urge which causes the emergence of apparent forms of beings is to be understood by the name *karma*. (*bhūta-bhavodbhava-karo visargaḥ karma-samjñitaḥ*).

This *karma,* according to the *Gītā*, takes place in the imperishable Reality (*akṣaram*), none other than the *akṣaram* of the present Upaniṣadic verse. The one Reality, when thought of as the Imperishable (*akṣaram*) Its spontaneous and invincible creative self-expression is called *karma*; whereas when thought of as pure Consciousness, the same creativity is Its flaming. The impressions such as 'my knowledge', 'your knowledge', 'his knowledge', subjective knowledge, objective knowledge, the tripartite factors of known-knower-knowledge, and so on, are all flames arising in the unbounded fire of pure Consciousness.

Aṇu, equivalent to the modern scientific concept of atom, means that which is indivisibly small. That which is formed of limbs alone is divisible and measurable. If at all the substance that underlies all that is divisible and measurable, is to be described in terms of divisibility and measurability, then it can be said that it is smaller than the smallest and larger than the largest, and is immeasurable, concepts very dear to almost all the basic source books of Vadānta (Cf. *Bhagavad Gītā,* VIII. 9).

That worlds are many is acceptable to modern scientists as well as to ancient *ṛṣi*s, though in relation to two different frames of reference. The world, as held by both, is what is perceived. One Sanskrit word for world is *loka*, meaning 'that which can be looked at', that which is perceptible. A perceivable is so only when there is a perceiver to perceive it. Unless perceived by a perceiver it will not be a 'perceived' and thus is inconceivable.

The perceiver and the perceived belong to a particular context of the flaming of the one Consciousness, in the form of the unfolding of its *karma* of perceiving, all meaningless in the absence of the flaming Reality. The perceiver and the perceived in fact form part of the overall flaming of the Reality, and the same Reality underlies both their substances. This is the reason why their mutual contact always results in the igniting of that common basis, consciousness in essence, in the form of a perception. In this way Indian psychologists explain the event of perception. A perceiver's perceiving an object results in the forgoing of the conditionings that caused the preceiver and the preceived to appear as separate, and it is the event of their inherent oneness actually becoming revealed that becomes a conscious experience. Though a non-dual experience in essence, we in our ignorance, register it as merely sense perception.

That consciousness, the substratum of all such flamings, is imperishable (*akṣaram*). My consciousness is short-lived, so is yours, but the one Consciousness common in all, the one Consciousness that flames as all, is ever-lasting. This ever-lasting Consciouness is none other than *Bahman*, literally the ever-growing.

It is the same one Consciousness that flames in each of us as *prāṇa,* the vital principle. As part of our attempt to know that Reality, we hear words of instruction on *Brahman*, and ponder on such instructions in our minds. Such words and their meanings, such ponderings and the ideas formulated, are all nothing but various apparent forms of the flaming of the one and only Consciousness. Even the life-principle in each living being is none other than That. The very same Reality appears as the world (*loka*) and the onlooker of *loka* is called *lokin*. The English word 'look' and the Sanskrit word *loka* are apparently derived from a common root. *Brahman,* the substance that assumes the form of all experiences, the experiencer and the experienced, is therefore not to be searched for externally. Even as a wave, looking at itself, sees itself as not apart from ocean, each experiencer has only to look within to see himself as that Reality in essence. Such interiorization of the search for Reality is here likened to the shooting of an arrow at a target. It is a method of enquiry unlike that of pursuing an object in a linear, logical way. The Reality searched for being none other than the seaker's own essential content, he merely has to make himself into an arrow to be shot at the target, the Absolute. The next verse gives more details of this shooting process. Linear, logical thinking culminates in our mind grasping a clear notion of the object searched for, whereas in the present method of enquiry, the enquirer, as an arrow, reaches the target and becomes one with it.

धनुर् गृहीत्वौपनिषदं महास्त्रं शरं ह्युपासानिशितं सन्धयीत ।
आयम्य तद्भावगतेन चेतसा लक्ष्यं तदेवाक्षरं सोम्य विद्धि ॥ ३ ॥

dhanur gṛhītvaupaniṣadaṁ mahāstraṁ
śaraṁ hyupāsāniśitaṁ sandhayīta ।
āyamya tad bhāvagatena cetasā
lakṣyaṁ tad evākṣaraṁ somya viddhi ॥ 3 ॥

Holding the great Upaniṣadic weapon as bow firmly
Should one put on to it the arrow
Sharpened by intense contemplative self-effort.
Pulling the bowstring back, with consciousness lost in
That,
Hit at That, the imperishable Target, my dear.

Expertise in a sort of archery is the means for attaining Immortality. The bow to be used is a great one, well-known in all the Upaniṣads; what it is will be stated in the next verse. The necessity of holding it firmly indicates the unavoidability of banking on it for the final attainment.

The arrow to be let fly — what it is will be shown in the next verse — is to be well sharpened at the whetstone of intense contemplative self-effort called *upāsanā*. Literally meaning to sit nearby and do service, *upāsanā* is a familiar word to religious people and seekers alike. With the former it means to sit nearby one's object of worship and to do service to it, which includes worshipping, singing in praise, meditating and so forth. A seeker's *upāsanā* involves sitting near his *guru* and serving him. Reference to the special qualities of such seekers is to be found in various parts of the scriptures in various contexts. These were gathered and systematized by Śaṅkara in his *Vivekacūḍāmaṇi* (The Crest-Jewel of Discrimination) and were together named *sādhana-catuṣṭaya-sampatti* (the state of being endowed with four prerequisites). The four are *nitya-anitya-viveka* (ability to discriminate the eternal from the transient), *vairāgya* (sense of detachment from the transient), the six instrumental self-disciplines that begin with *śama*, and *mumukṣutva* (intense yearning for final Liberation). The six items (beginning with *śama*) are *śama* (tranquillity), *dama* (self-restraint), *uparati* (abstinence), *titikṣā* (endurance), *śraddhā* (faith) and *samādhāna* (to see *Brahman* alone as the sole goal and sole refuge in life). The Yoga system, on the other hand, systematizes the prerequisites on the part of a seeker in a different way, classifying them as *yama* and *niyama*, the former more physical, the latter more mental.

Yama consists of five items, namely, *ahiṁsā* (non-hurting), *satyam* (honesty), *asteyam* (non-stealing), *brahmacarya* (continence), and *aparigraha* (having no possessions); *śauca* (purity and honesty), *saṁtoṣa* (contentment), *tapas* (austerity), *svādhyāya* (self-learning) and *īśvarapraṇidhāna* (meditating and worshipping God) are the five items under *niyama,* meaning self-restraint. Irrespective of the system one follows, self-restraint, both physical and mental, as well as uncompromising self-effort towards the final attainment constitute the essential prerequisites on the part of a seeker, all implicit in the word *upāsanā* of the present verse.

An arrow's force in the art of archery depends on the extent to which the bowstring is pulled backwards. The pulling backwards in the present case shows the necessity of withdrawal and interiorization of the search, made clear already in the last verse. This way of search for Reality, in India, is known as *nivṛtti-mārga* (the path of withdrawal) as against *pravṛtti-mārga* (the path of external activity). This pulling backwards of the bowstring has to be at its optimum.

Along with this pulling back of the bowstring should be the proper aiming of the arrow. That is to say, the withdrawal from the external and the interiorization of the search has to go side by side with the positive and accurate aiming of the arrow at the Imperishable *Puruṣa*, each making the other more effective and purposeful, both together resulting in the final accomplishment.

It is with the full awareness that what appears as words and mind, i.e., as the bow, arrow, the art of archery, are all various manifest forms of the one and the same *Puruṣa* sought, that the arrow is to be aimed at and shot at. The consciousness of the archer in that state could be said to be fully attuned to and lost in That, the Imperishable *Puruṣa*. The Guru's instruction here is to shoot and hit the target with the archer's mind already totally absorbed in the target (*tad-bhāva-gatena cestasā*).

प्रणवो धनुः शरो ह्यात्मा ब्रह्म तल्लक्ष्यमुच्यते ।
अप्रमत्तेन वेद्धव्यं शरवत् तन्मयो भवेत् ॥ ४ ॥

praṇavo dhanuḥ śaro hy ātmā brahma tal laksyam ucyate ।
apramattena veddhavyaṁ śaravat tanmayo bhavet ॥ 4 ॥

Praṇava is the bow, and oneself the arrow;
Brahman spoken of as That, is the target.
Unerringly is It to be shot at,
And, like an arrow, should come to be one with That.

That the Upaniṣadic weapon mentioned in the last verse is none other than *praṇava*, another name for *AUṀ*, is made clear in this verse. It literally means, that which is of undiminishing novelty. *AUṀ* is the monosyllable that signifies the Absolute, *ātman*. God in the Sanskrit language, and realizing it as the significance of life is an ever new experience. The key notion on which are pivoted the teachings of all the Upaniṣads, *AUṀ* is the one veritable tool acceptable to all the Indian schools of thought and all seekers. The *Māṇḍūkya Upaniṣad* is meant solely for expounding the significance of this most mystical of all sounds.

Repeating this syllable a number of times is a popular spiritual practice among devout seekers — the practice known as *japa*, equivalent to telling one's beads. *Japa*, strictly speaking, means, to have both verbal and mental clarity simultaneously (*japa vyaktāyām vāci mānase ca*). The making use of *praṇava* as the chief weapon as understood in the present context, however, involves even more than this *japa*. Constant cogitation on its significance as expounded in the *Māṇḍūkya* and other Upaniṣads, along with meditating on it, eventually results in gaining the inner transparency of life's signifance. It is this trasparency that whets the weapon of *praṇava* and sharpens it.

The arrow is the self (*ātman*), the whole being of the seeker himself, true to the etymological sense of the word. *Ātman* is not merely the soul or the principle that animates one's body, as is popularly conceived. If taken in this latter sense, the bodily part of existence would then have no place in *Brahman*'s existence — the one Reality where bodily and mental aspects of appearance are inseparably one, being different manifestations of the One. The seeker, therefore, when he transforms himself into the arrow to be aimed and to hit *Brahman*, has to involve his whole being, without making himself subject to any artificial division as between body and soul or matter and mind. And unerring should be the aiming of the self-arrow, and it is to make this unerringness certain that the arrow is to be kept constantly sharp through *upāsanā*.

An arrow shot out hits at its target and gets held there, becoming one with it. The seeker also, shooting himself as the arrow, becomes well embedded into the target — *Brahman* — and becomes one with it. The shooting out and hitting at the *Brahman*-target simply signifies a sudden shift that occurs in the vision of the seeker. In the place of seeing himself as an independently exisiting being with his own free will, as he did before, he sends himself forth to be one with *Brahman*, to merge with *Brahman*. Thenceforward he sees himself only as *Brahman*, his own existence and will undifferentiable from those of *Brahman*: even before attaining this new enlightenment and acquiring this new attitude to life, he in reality was already one with *Brahman*, without knowing it; now his oneness with *Brahman* is known to him and that makes all the difference. The occurrence of sudden change is only in his vision, which in no way affects what really is.

यस्मिन् द्यौः पृथिवी चान्तरिक्षमोतं मनः सह प्राणैश्च सर्वैः ।
तमेवैकं जानथ आत्मानमन्या वाचो विमुञ्चथामृतस्यैष सेतुः ।। ५ ।।

yasmin dyauḥ pṛthivī cāntarikṣam otaṁ
manaḥ saha prāṇaiśca sarvaiḥ ।
tam evaikaṁ jānatha ātmānam
anyā vāco vimuñcatha amṛtasyaiṣa setuḥ ।। 5 ।।

He into whom are woven the sky, the earth and the interspace,
And also mind along with all the *prāṇa*s,
Know Him alone as yourself;
And do dismiss all else,
He alone is the bridge to Immortality.

The focus in this verse is on what the seeker, who finds himself embedded in *Brahman*, the target, sees. This attainment of getting embedded in *Brahman* could be likened to a pin's becoming aware of itself as being steel in essence, and, forgoing its identity with its bodily aspect, i.e., the pin-form, realizing "I am steel". The seeker, likewise, forgoing his individuating conditioning factors, turns to the essential content in himself with intense meditative contemplation. In other words, the focus turns from appearance to Reality.

A pin, identifying itself with steel, sees steel not only as having the apparent form of the pin, but as having the appearance of knives, various tools, all machinery and even the enormous Golden Gate Bridge. The pin realizes, "Such is the steel I am". It will see all such apparent forms woven into itself. The seeker, likewise, seeing himself as one with *Brahman*, will see all the worlds — the earth, the heaven, the mid-region — woven into the very same Reality. All the tools, utensils, machines and the Golden Gate Bridge rely on the steel-substance for their existence; all the worlds and the individuating factors in the seeker himself, such as mind, vitality, senses, physical organs and so on, rely on the one Reality — *Brahman* — for their respective apparent forms. All of them are thus woven into that one *Brahman*.

Many are the theories, hypotheses and opinions that prevail concerning what is real. Such multiplicity of theories and opinions in no way makes the real they supposedly try to reveal, many. All the theories and opinions are based on certain of the apparent aspects of what is real and they always necessarily differ according to the apparent aspects they are based on. Those who intuitively see what is real do not formulate any theory or opinion about it, and therefore there is no difference of opinion between them either. Wherever there is disagreement, therefore, there is surely lack of vision of the real. One who knows the real, with no theorizing about it, simply visualizes it as his own beingness, realizing his inseparable oneness with it, even as a wave finds its oneness with the ocean.

The reality that underlies all apparent forms is imperishable. Forms such as pins, knives, machines, for example, are all perishable whereas their one underlying steel is imperishable. So too the imperishability of the underlying reality in all of us. That Reality — *Brahman* — is immortal. The highest of all human aspirations is to attain immortality, and the only way to attain this is to realize one's inseparable oneness with the Immortal *Brahman*. This awareness, this realization, releases one from the fear of death and makes immortality an accomplished fact. This is the bridge made from mortality to immortality.

With the arrow — oneself — having hit the target — *Brahman* — one gets totally stabilized oneself therein, perceiving all the worlds, and oneself also with all the transactions and functions taking place in oneself, as multifarious, changeful manifest forms of the one and only *Brahman*, dismissing all prevailing, contending theories and opinions. Such is , or such should be, the state of one who, as an arrow, has hit its target.

अरा इव रथनाभौ संहता यत्र नाड्यः स एषोऽन्तश्चरते बहुधा जायमानः ।
ओमित्येवं ध्यायथ आत्मानं स्वस्ति वः पराय तमसः परस्तात् ॥ ६ ॥

arā iva rathanābhau saṁhatā yatra nāḍyaḥ
sa eṣo'ntaś carate bahudhā jāyamānaḥ ।
oṁ ityevaṁ dhyāyatha ātmānaṁ
svasti vaḥ parāya tamasaḥ parastāt ॥ 6 ॥

He, wherein all nerves meet together,
Like spokes in the hub of a wheel,
Being such, becoming multitudinous, lives and moves within everything.
Meditate therefore yourself as *AUṀ*.
May you succeed in crossing over to the shore farther from darkness.

The body of an organism can be divided into many sections and sub-sections, such as those of organs, tissues, cells, microbiological components, molecules, atoms, sub-atomic particles and so on, each having its own specific function, which ensure the existence and fulfil the function of the organism as a whole. The existence and function of the organism is more than the aggregate of its component parts. Those components and their existence are conceivable as coming together and finding a common ground in the wholeness of the organism and it is the organism as a whole that makes the existence and functions of the components meaningful. All sub-systems of existence find themselves united in one system, like spokes in the hub of a wheel.

Branching out of sub-systems within one cosmic system resembles the behaviour of the nervous system of a body. Nerve endings reach out to every cell of a body, yet remain centralized as one functional whole. The cosmic system, sometimes conceived of as a super-organism, whatever be the component entities and their respective functions, likewise belongs to a functional whole. This allegorical nervous system centralizes and interlinks not simply the physical entities in the cosmos, but whatever be the functions, known or unknown, mental, vital or physical, all are centralized in the one system of cosmic existence and life. Expressed otherwise, this entire system of existence and life, and all systems within it constitute the creative self-expression of the one and only *Brahman*, the Imperishable *Puruṣa*. It is this *Puruṣa* that lives and moves in and through all such phenomenal systems. Each constituent part of these phenomena, the seeker one among them, has to live fully aware of its oneness with the one Reality that lives and functions in it and as it.

Spokes of a wheel are well fixed on to its hub, and their ability to function as spokes depends on how firmly they are fixed to the hub. So too are the component parts of the world, including the seeker. To the extent he finds himself well fitted into the total immortal system, he finds peace, and attains immortality. To the extent he alienates himself from the totality and tries to be an entity existing on its own, he makes himself miserable, and impending death scares him. *Brahman* is the one hub into which are fitted all the sub-systems.

Yet in one respect the cosmic wheel differs from the chariot wheel. The hub of the latter is located at one point at its centre, whereas that of the former is everywhere within each and every apparent form *Brahman* assumes; it remains as the creative substance within and outside each entity in all the worlds. Yet like the invisibly moving central point of a wheel, it lives and moves invisibly and inconceivably in all visible and conceivable forms. The same steel substance it is that remains in each tool or machine, and makes each of them function in a different way, serving a different purpose. So too, the one invisible and imperishable *Puruṣa* lives and moves within (*antaś-carati*) everything visible, each serving a different purpose in the overall system. *AUṀ* is the sound that represents the one Reality.

AUṀ, in the present context of archery, was first conceived as the bow, the chief weapon or means to be utilized, but it is also the linguistic sign that represents *Brahman*, the target. Once the arrow has hit and embedded itself in the target, the seeker — the arrow — realizes that what exists is *Brahman* alone. What was formerly thought of as means separate from the end now turns out to be non-existent apart from the target reached, and thus ends and means find themselves inseparably one in the ultimate sense, the state that marks the final attainment conceived by Vedānta. The master's instruction to the seeker is to meditate on himself as *AUṀ* or *Brahman* in essence, where also the distinction between ends and means vanishes by itself.

Such meditation is the only way to cross over to the shore farther from darkness (*tamas*), the only bridge (*setu*) from mortality (*mṛtyu*) to immortality (*amṛta*). What really exists (*sat*) is *Brahman* alone, the Immortal Reality, Pure Consciousness (*Puruṣa*), pure effulgence (*jyotiḥ*) in essence. Mere manifestations of *Brahman*, whatever else is thought of as existing, have no real existence of their own, and thus are non-existent (*asat*). The darkness (*tamas*) in short stands for non-existence (*asat*) and mortality (*mṛtyuḥ*) also. The Master's instruction thus reminds us of the famous words of the *Bṛhadāraṇyaka Upaniṣad* — *asato mā sad gamaya, tamaso mā jyotir gamaya, mṛtyor mā amṛtam gamaya* (May I be led on from non-existence to Existence, from darkness to effulgence, from mortality to immortality).

Svasti, the word of greeting in the Sanskrit language, means well-being, or more correctly, 'well-founded existence'. There is no better way to be well-founded than to find oneself already founded in *Brahman*, the Immortal Reality, Pure Effulgence in essence (*sat-jyotiḥ-amṛtaḥ*), that which the Master wishes for his disciple here.

यः सर्वज्ञः सर्वविद् यस्यैष महिमा भुवि ।
दिव्ये ब्रह्मपुरे ह्येष व्योम्न्यात्मा प्रतिष्ठितः ।।
मनोमयः प्राणशरीरनेता प्रतिष्ठितोऽन्ने हृदयं सन्निधाय ।
तद् विज्ञानेन परिपश्यन्ति धीरा आनन्दरूपममृतं यद् विभाति ।। ७ ।।

yaḥ sarvajñaḥ sarva-vid yasyaiṣa mahimā bhuvi ।
divye brahma-pure hy eṣa vyomny ātmā pratīṣṭhitaḥ ।।
manomayaḥ prāṇa-śarīra-netā
pratiṣṭhito'nne hṛdayaṁ sannidhāya ।
tad vijñānena paripaśyanti dhīrā
ānanda-rūpaṁ amṛtaṁ yad vibhāti ।। 7 ।।

He is all-knowledge and all-knowing,
Whose greatness is what appears as this world.
In the firmament of the effulgent city of *Brahman*
Is the Self well-founded.
He appears as mind,
He appears as the controller of *prāṇa*s and body.
With heart well-placed in food is He well-founded.
The inflexibly wise visualizes Him holistically,
Perceiving Him in all the specific forms,
Immortal *ānanda* in essence,
Manifesting specifically as all.

The arrow's meditative self-perception, on its hitting the target and getting embedded in it, was portrayed in the last verse. Now this verse focuses on the arrow's — the seeker's — experience of its own state on the fulfilment of that meditation.

He finds himself well-stabilized in the city of *Brahman*. The essence of the great dictum, *ayam ātmā brahma* (this self is *Brahman* indeed) is now thus a direct experience for him. He sees himself as all-knowledge and all-knowing. What was in the beginning (Verse I.i.9) related to as the object of enquiry of *parā-vidyā* (transcendental wisdom) thus becomes an accomplished fact for the seeker. *Sarvajña*, translated as 'all-knowledge', is the one who perceives one substance — Pure Consciousness — alone as Real. *Sarva-vit* (the all-knowing), on the other hand, is he who perceives all apparent forms distinctly with the awareness that they are all merely manifestations of the one and only Substance. The two perceptions, like the two sides of a coin, are mutually complementary.

The glory and greatness of the Reality he finds himself in is what appears as and fills the being of the world he perceives. He, in other words, sees himself and the world he is in as none other than the non-apparent glory of the one Reality become apparent. This Reality being *Brahman*, Its glory become apparent is *Brahma-pura*, the city of *Brahman*, wherein he finds himself well-stabilized. As the one who dwells in a city (*pura*) he is now *puruṣa* (the city-dweller) and the city being effulgent or rather effulgence in essence (*divya*), so too is he. Comparable only to the effulgent firmament, the reason why it is at times termed *cidākāśa* (the firmament of consciousness), it is as in it, as one with it, and as part of that effulgence, that the seeker sees himself and the world.

An individual, while being one with that One Reality, retains his individuality, owing to the conditioning factors such as bodily form, senses, mind, intellect, the animating vitality and so on, all together known as *upādhis* in Vedānta. On the fulfilment of the meditation, the seeker, already embedded in the Reality, finds it transparently clear that all such conditioning factors, his resultant individuality, the individualities of all entities like him, are all phenomena appearing as the self-expression of the creative urge inherent in the very same Reality, and that none of them has existence apart from That. The *ātmā* (self), as is apparent here, is not the animating principle or soul in the body (though often misconceived so), which specifically is termed *prāṇa* here. The self is oneself, whereas the soul is possessed by one. *Ātmā* is the substance that gets individuated as each being, whose subtlest apparent form is *prāṇa* (soul) and the grossest, body.

The most basic of all yearnings in every individual living being is for happiness. The same is true for the individual already embedded in *Brahman*. This happiness, to be elicited from one's own being, is not to be derived from something else, as is often conceived. As the individuation of a being from the one substance needs certain conditioning factors such as body, so too the actualization of happiness, the eliciting of happiness from oneself, needs certain instrumental conditioning factors: the subject and the object, referred to in the verse as *hṛdayam* (heart) and *annam* (food). The latter term connotes inclusively all that is enjoyable, the whole world, whose existence is nowhere else than in *Brahman*, as *Brahman*. That underlying Reality that unfolds as *annam* or the object of enjoyment on the one hand and as *hṛdayam* or the enjoying subject on the other, together instrumental in the actualization of happiness within, is what is implicit in the word *ānanda*, usually translated as 'Happiness' or 'Bliss'. In the *sat-cit-ānanda* content of the Self , *ānanda* is the value sense of consciousness that evaluates each experience, whatever it may be, as pleasurable, painful or indifferent. It is this content of the Self that unfolds positively as pleasure and negatively as pain. This actualization of the *ānanda* content of the Self, either in the form of pleasure or pain, occurs with the instrumentality of *annam* and *hṛdayam* aspects of appearance. Food when consumed evokes happiness, for the *ānanda* content of *Brahman* is the substance that fills the being of both the enjoyer and the food enjoyed.

Knowing this basic Reality, one sees the one implicit immortal *ānanda* as explicit in all momentary pleasures and pains. On seeing a certain manifest form of *ānanda* in all pleasures and pains, one can remain neutral towards both — considered as a *yogī*'s state in the *Bhagavad Gītā*. His wisdom thus keeps him firm and he is then a *dhīra* (inflexibly wise).

भिद्यते हृदयग्रन्थिश्छिद्यन्ते सर्वसंशयाः ।
क्षीयन्ते चास्य कर्माणि तस्मिन् दृष्टे परावरे ॥ ८ ॥

bhidyate hṛdaya-granthiś chidyante sarva-saṁśayāḥ ।
kṣīyante cāsya karmāṇi tasmin dṛṣṭe parāvare ॥ 8 ॥

The knots of heart shatter,
All doubts get dispelled,
And all deeds (*karma*s) get exhausted,
On visualizing Him — the transcendental and the
immanent.

Experiencing the contentment of being fully liberated from all bondages and obligations — the state known as *mukti* or *mokṣa*, both meaning liberatedness — is the ultimate value of the vision depicted in these verses. Otherwise one finds oneself tied up to various obligations — to one's family, kith and kin, race, religion, state, ideas and ideologies, traditions and customs, and so on. All these bondages are emotional in essence. The seat of all emotions, as conceived by Indian psychologists, is one's heart, bondages likened to knots having been formed in the 'arteries' around it. Liberated, one feels all such knots are dissolved and it is then one finds that that liberation, attained through knowing one's own self-content, is the real meaning of life. All other values, until then thought of as making life meaningful, suddenly reveal themselves as life's conditioning bonds and seem like knots in the arteries around one's own heart.

Our emotions are given vent to through our efforts, either to please those to whom we feel emotionally attached or to possess them. Such efforts, called *karmas*, could either be bodily, verbal or even mental. Behind each *karma* is the notion,"I am the doer of it", and so "Any benefit therefrom should also be mine". Doing evil deeds, one becomes scared of having to eat their bitter fruits, and this fear mostly tempts one to perform expiatory deeds, known as *parihāra-karma*, making one more attached to more *karmas*, thus forming a vicious circle with no way out. The only way to rescue oneself from this predicament is to realise one's own existence as one with the existence of the totality of nature and one's *karmas* as part of the total movement of nature, seeing oneself thus as not the doer of actions while still engaged in actions as part of nature's activity. The real doer of actions is nature alone which, active by nature, has no sense of agency. As part of this active nature, man likewise should not feel any sense of agency in action. An action with no sense of agency behind it, is, in effect, no action (*karma*) at all, and thus one finds one's own actions as non-actions. The entire third chapter of the *Bhagavad Gītā* attempts to clarify how this is to be actualized in life.

This liberatedness, as is often misconceived by religious practitioners or believers, is not an other-worldly experience nor is it to be actualized in the hereafter. No Transcendental wisdom (*parā*) is to be actualized in the hereafter. It is to be actualized and experienced in the here and now (*avara*). No self-knowledge being possible while one is not oneself, its final result — liberation — is also not experienceable while one is not oneself. One remins oneself only in the here and now, the anterior and posterior states of existence of what is real in one remaining quite indistinct and unknowable. Being engaged in one's natural activities as part of nature's activities is also relevant only in the here and now; liberation from all *karmas* and resultant bondages are thus meaningful in the here and now alone, the reason why the vision of Reality, as stated here, is at the same time transcendent and immanent. How the two aspects of existence — the eternal Reality and the transitory appearances — are inseparably one here and now, we have already clarified under Verse II.i.2.

हिरण्मये परे कोशे विरजं ब्रह्म निष्कलम् ।
तच्छुभ्रं ज्योतिषां ज्योतिस्तद् यदात्मविदो विदुः ॥ ९ ॥

hiraṇmaye pare kośe virajaṁ brahma niṣkalam ।
tacchubhraṁ jyotiṣāṁ jyotis tad yad ātmavido viduḥ ॥ 9 ॥

In the Transcendental golden treasury
Is *Brahman*, the actionless and partless;
Pure is It, the Light of lights,
What the self-knowers perceive.

The Golden Veil

It is an idiom characteristic of Upaniṣads to say that *Brahman* is hidden within a golden casket or within a golden treasure-house. The *Īśa Upaniṣad*, for example, says:

> Veiled in a golden casket
> Is Reality's face. (Verse 15)

Here it is a golden treasury wherein *Brahman* is seen as hidden. Whether presented in words or conceived of as an idea, the Absolute Reality has two conceivable aspects: the eternal aspect of being the Substance (*sat*) and the transitory aspect of appearance (*bhāva*). Stated as two and conceived as two though, the two remain inseparably one in actuality, even as gold and ornament always remain inseparable. Those prone to abstraction think of *sat* (the eternal, abstract Substance) as real; whereas those whose bias favours apparent forms consider transitory appearances, emerging and merging constantly and constituting the world, as real. The former could be called idealists, the latter materialists. Yet we know, without an eternal substance no transitory form appears and without assuming a transitory, apparent form of some kind no abstract substance exists. Gold, in itself indestructible, does not exist without assuming some destructible form, and no ornament form emerges without gold as its substance. Intuitively perceiving the non-duality of the two, of the eternal substance and the transitory form — of the eternal *Brahman* and transitory worlds — is what makes one a philosopher (*tattva-darśin*) as the *Bhagavad Gītā* underlines in its Verse II.16. Only such a philosopher perceives the world, his personal existence and life along with all its problems intuitively, all inseparably one with *Brahman*. This inconceivable yet actual non-duality is the secret treasure hidden in the golden treasury or casket, with the two conceivable eternal and transitory aspects for its two halves.

Whatever is verbally represented, whatever is conceived of as ideas, eventually ends up as a mere casket encasing the real gem of non-duality, or the side-walls of the golden treasury wherin the real treasure is securely stored. Those who consider *Brahman* merely as the transcendental (*parā*), abstract Substance that underlies all appearances, do not perceive the truly Real. What they perceive as Real is merely the golden casket or treasury wherein the real treasure is to be found. They remain satisfied on seeing its golden gleam — the beauty of words or sublimity of ideas — while not knowing the Real Treasure hidden inside. To open the casket and see directly what is inside is not possible even for an earnest seeker without the Grace of the very same Treasure or of one's Guru. The seeker of the *Īśa Upaniṣad* therfore prays God, following the words quoted above:

> O *Pūṣan*, open it out for me,
> The righteous seeker. (Verse15)

All that is luminous in all the worlds, the next verse will say, is so because of the effulgence of *Brahman*. Even the words of the Upaniṣads and their meanings are luminous because of *Brahman*, the very reality they supposedly reveal, and for this reason, no word, even of the Upaniṣads, the present Upaniṣad no exception, is capable of making *Brahman* its meaning. Upaniṣads, to teach *Brahmavidyā* (the science of *Brahman*), instead of revealing it, present us with *Brahman* beautifully wrapped up in poetically sublime word symbols. To uncover it and see what is hidden within is the subtlest of all spiritual practices following the Upaniṣadic approach. The Upaniṣads, the word itself meaning secret teaching, therefore do not reveal the secret of the teaching directly.

Actionless, Partless, Pure

Emotionless and changeless as it is, *Brahman* however is the Reality in which appear and disappear all emotions and changes, the sense in which It is actionless (*viraja*). All actions and emotions are effected by *rajo-guṇa* (the active modality of nature) and as that which is devoid of the *rajo-guṇa*, along with all the other *guṇas*, *Brahman* is *viraja*.

Kalā is any small part of a whole, where the whole is more than the sum of parts. Having no parts, *Brahman* is even more than such a whole; It is simply partless (*niṣkala*).

Colour always signifies the inherent quality of anything, and *śubhram* is the state of having no colour whatsoever. Though giving rise to all that has qualities, *Brahman* in itself is qualityless and thus colourless. *Śubhram* also means whiteness which, though achromatic, is the aggregate of all chromatic colours and even more than the sum of those colours. So too, *Brahman*, by itself qualityless, diffracts into all entities and their qualities, needing no prism.

The Light of Lights

Another idiom dear to all scriptures, the Light of lights, as understood here, is not merely the light that illuminates all the luminaries such as the sun, the moon, stars, fire and so on. Whether such luminaries do exist or not would be meaningless in the absence of a seeing consciousness. The entire universe is a functional system; every minute part of it has a role of its own to fulfil in keeping it going. The fulfilment of the life purpose of each of its constituent elements is so structured that each helps fulfil the existence and purpose of existence of all else that surrounds it, all interlinked and belonging to a deep ecosystem. A mango tree in bloom, for example, attracts bees. They in their turn enjoy sucking honey from the flowers while fulfilling the purpose of the flowering of the tree, through pollination. Mangoes, when ripe, are relished by birds, animals and humans alike, which relishing itself fulfils the tree's purpose of dispersing its seeds to far off places to grow on their own. The earth, water, air and other elements that surround the tree, if conscious,— it has of course been proved that they are conscious — should feel the contentment of having played their respective roles in making the existence and happiness of the mango tree, bees, birds, animals, humans and other beings, possible. Life system is so organized that one's existence helps ensure the existence of another, one's happiness helps ensure the happiness of another. The deep-seated urge for happiness, one of the signs of life, is actualized by the interlinking of one's means with another's ends, and one's ends with another's means. It is thus in the web of Happiness (*ānanda*) that life in the deep ecosystem is interlinked, all systematized by an all-knowing

Consciousness, none other than that which we are concerned with here, *Brahman*, pure effulgence in essence. The sun's role of radiating light and energy on to the earth making life possible on it could be conceived of as part of the planning of that one Consciousness; so too is the role of everything else. *Brahman* is thus the Light of all lights. The *Kena Upaniṣad*, going into more details, says, It is the Eye of eyes, the Ear of ears, the Mind of mind, the *Prāṇa* of *prāṇa*s and so on (vide Verse 2 to 9). We have attempted to make this point clearer in our comments on that Upaniṣad.

Ātma-vit

A knower of the Self is known as *ātma-jñānin* or *ātma-vit*, which words imply that what he knows is *ātman*. Every discipline has a well-specified field of enquiry of its own which defines the object to be clearly known by pursuing that particular discipline, such as micro-biology, sub-atomic physics, chemistry, bio-chemistry and so on. But the field of enquiry in the present instance is not such a well-defined one, for it is the effulgence that illuminates all, including oneself, the Substance that appears as all, including oneself. Its knower intuitively perceives the one all-pervading Reality by seeing himself as pervaded by it, where the subject becomes the object, and the object the subject. This is an enlightenment where the duality of subject and object merges in the effulgence of one beingness; it is not a knowledge *about* something. The *ātma-vit* is therefore not a person who knows *ātman* as an object; rather he is the one who finds himself merged in what he knows.

न तत्र सूर्यो भाति न चन्द्रतारकं नेमा विद्युतो भान्ति कुतोऽयमग्निः।
तमेव भान्तमनुभाति सर्वं तस्य भासा सर्वमिदं विभाति ।। १० ।।

na tatra sūryo bhāti na candratārakaṁ
nemā vidyuto bhānti kuto'yam agniḥ ।
tam eva bhāntam anubhāti sarvaṁ
tasya bhāsā sarvam idaṁ vibhāti ।। 10 ।।

The Sun illumines It not, nor the moon and stars;
These lightnings illumine It not, much less this fire!
Following Its shining indeed all is luminous;

By Its light it is that everything specifically shines.

The depiction of the experience the arrow — the seeker — has on hitting and getting embedded in the target continues, showing the reverse side of the picture from the last verse. The nature of the Reality he finds himself in becomes fully transparent to him, yet it is unlike the clarity he gains in his attempts to understand anything else.

An object, for example, is made visible to eyes by the sunlight or some other light. Yet the Reality that conceived and formulated the sense organ eye, with its ability to perceive all objects distinctly in the presence of external lights like the sun, the moon, lightning, fire, turns out to be an internal experience, never shone on by the luminaries nor is It perceived by eyes. It, consciousness in essence, shines assuming the forms of the luminaries, of all that is illumined by them, and of the shining sense organ. The world experienced thus becomes apparent. The arrow — the seeker, one of the entities illumined by the one causal Effulgence — finds himself, like everything else, a luminous aspect of that one wondrous Effulgence.

ब्रह्मैवेदममृतं पुरस्ताद् ब्रह्म पश्चाद् ब्रह्म दक्षिणतश्चोत्तरेण ।
अधश्चोर्ध्वं च प्रसृतम् ब्रह्मैवेदं विश्वमिदं वरिष्ठम् ।। ११ ।।

brahmaivedam amṛtaṁ purastād
brahma paścād brahma dakṣiṇataṣcottareṇa ।
adhaś cordhvaṁ ca prasṛtaṁ brahmai
vedaṁ viśvam idaṁ variṣṭham ।। 11 ।।

Brahman indeed is all this!
It is the Immortal!
Brahman before, *Brahman* behind, to the right, to the left too!
It spreads forth below and above!
Brahman, the best of desirables, indeed, is this whole world!

The seeker's — the arrow's — summarization of what he experiences, this verse is meant to be understood, is understandable, without any comment. He sees *Brahman* alone everywhere, himself absorbed into It.

MUṆḌAKA III

Khaṇḍa 1

DIFFERENTATING *parā-vidyā* and *aparā-vidyā*, the first *Muṇḍaka* of this Upaniṣad showed that those who are intent on Liberation take to the former *vidyā* alone. The first section of the second *Muṇḍaka* spoke of *Brahman* as the causal substance of all the worlds, they themselves not existing apart from *Brahman*. We, in our day-to-day life, remain unaware of our oneness with *Brahman,* and think of ourselves as living our own life, resulting in all sorts of worries, conflicts, trials and tribulations. The way to realize our oneness with *Brahman* and thus rid ourselves of all problems, was the subject dealt with in the second section of the second *Muṇḍaka*. Transforming ourselves into an arrow to be shot at *Brahman* with *AUṀ* for bow was recommended as the means. The present third *Muṇḍaka*, in its first section, explores the mysteriousness of the *Brahman* one finds oneself one with, showing how It is, when logically viewed all paradox.

द्वा सुपर्णा सयुजा सखाया समानं वृक्षं परिषस्वजाते ।
तयोरन्यः पिप्पलं स्वाद्वत्त्यनश्नन्नन्यो अभिचाकशीति ।। १ ।।

dvā suparṇā sayujā sakhāyā
samānaṁ vṛkṣaṁ pariṣasvajāte ।
tayor anyaḥ pippalaṁ svādvatty
anaśnan anyo abhicākaśīti ।। 1 ।।

Two beautiful winged-ones, fast bound companions,
Cling to the selfsame tree.
Of the two, the one eats delicious berries
While the other looks on, not eating.

The famous allegory of two birds perching on the selfsame tree, one relishing delicious berries while the other just looking on, is what the present section of the Upaniṣad begins with. Both, beautifully winged and having the same name, are fast-bound companions, never remaining apart. The same allegory is found verbatim in the *Śvetāśvatara-Upaniṣad* (Verse IV.6), and there is a reference to it in the *Cūlika Upaniṣad* (Verse 8).

More well-known than the bird analogy is the tree analogy in almost all scriptures. In the Bible, for example, the Book of Job (14.7-9) depicts a life-tree. The *Bhagavad Gītā*, at the beginning of its fifteenth chapter, portrays the picture of an undecaying fig-tree with roots hidden in the higher worlds and branches growing downwards, the Vedic verses forming its leaves. The last chapter of the *Kaṭha Upaniṣad* also begins with the description of a similar tree. Narayana Guru's depiction in two contexts of his *Ātmopadeśa-śatakam* (One Hundred Verses of Self-Instruction) of a *māyā*-tree overgrown by two intertwining creepers also derives from nature. Slightly at variance might be the deep singificance of the imagery in each context though, a common structural pattern indubitably acceptable to all seers is evident in all of them. In the unique unity of life do meet its unknown source factors hidden high above all knowledge and the endlessly branching knowables, the latter symbolized in the *Bhagavad Gītā* by the Vedic verses. In the realm of knowledge, its subjective aspect branches out endlessly as the world of concepts, and the objective aspect too branches out exactly the same way as the world of percepts, both together making the functional consciousness structurally perfect. Life is the trunk wherein meet the two endlessly branching realms. Such is life seen in its entirety.

It is in this life-tree that the two birds are nesting : One the 'I-sense' always considering itself as the doer of actions, enjoyer of fruits and the knower of things, and the other the witnessing consciousness. Each one of us, finding oneself in the life-tree, thinks oneself to be in contact with the external objects, as knowing each entity distinctly, as doing all necessary actions moment by moment, and as the enjoyer of objects and of the fruits of one's own actions. In reality all these take place as part of the beginningless and endless flow of nature (*prakṛti*). This 'I-sense', separate in each individual, is the bird that relishes berries. Yet a witnessing consciousness is within all of us, always aware — "I am now in contact with the world", "I am now engaged in activities", "I am now enjoying", "I am now thinking ", and so on. This witnessing 'I', always remaining the same, changeless, is free of all attachments, unaffected by the inconstancy of the other. This witnessing consciousness in one individual is not in essence different from the one in another; it, in all beings, is one. It is the one Consciousness that witnesses everything that takes place in the whole world, in all the worlds. It sees everything as taking place within itself, as activated by itself.

What makes life beautiful and worth living is these two aspects of consciousness, always inseparable, one meaningless without the other. In the absence of life, the existence of the self, self- enquiry and even the existence of God, would all be meaningless, which is why the two birds are conceived of as perching on the self-same life-tree. Both could of course be termed 'I'. The 'I' in my notion, "I enjoy", is the first bird, whereas the 'I' in "I am aware of my enjoying" is the second one, each forming one half of the meaningfulness of life. To give a slightly different interpretation to the context, a seeker-disciple could be likened to the former bird and the knower-*guru* to the latter. The *kṣara* and *akṣara* (perishable and imperishable) *puruṣa*s conceived of at the beginning of the last section could also be thought of as another version of the two birds.

समाने वृक्षे पुरूषो निमग्नोऽनीशया शोचति मुह्यमानः ।
जुष्टं यदा पश्यत्यन्यमीशमस्य महिमानमिति वीतशोकः ।। २ ।।

samāne vṛkṣe puruṣo nimagno'
nīśayā śocati muhyamānaḥ ।
juṣṭam yadā paśyati anyam īśam
asya mahimānam iti vītaśokaḥ ।। 2 ।।

On the selfsame tree, the one *puruṣa*
Engrossed as he is in eating,
Finding himself not its controller,
Gets confused and grieves.
Seeing the other, the controller, contented,
He becomes devoid of sorrow,

Wondering, "How Great He is! "

Speculation based on the bird-and-tree-analogy continues: the bird engrossed in eating the berries of the tree — every individual 'I' engrossed in enjoying all that is enjoyable in the world — is termed *puruṣa*, following the nomenclature preferred throughout the body of this Upaniṣad. The other bird — the witnessing 'I' — will also be termed *puruṣa* in the next verse, clarifying that the two birds represent the *kṣara-puruṣa* and *akṣara-puruṣa* seen at the beginning, all notions added to them later being only embellishments.

Īśa and Anīśa

Īśa, though the Sanskrit word for God, literally means, 'the controller'. One in control of something is its *Īśa*. Everyone engrossed in enjoying life objectively longs to make the enjoyable object their own and also to keep the way of enjoying it under their own control. The more one longs the more one finds oneself not in control either of the object or of the manner of enjoying it. Frustrated, one starts thinking of the meaning of life, and gets confused as to what gives real happiness, or even what happiness is.

Mostly with the aid of a guide — a *guru* — and rarely on his own, the seeker turns to himself and sees himself as worried and also aspiring towards a meaningful happiness, both known to 'him'. The one 'he' who knows both is neither worried nor has aspirations; it, fully contented, simply witnesses both. This contented 'I' is seen by him in the selfsame life-tree, but affected in no way by its inconsistencies and impermanence. Seeing it in himself, he is filled with wonder, "How Great He is!" Really that 'Great He' in oneself is the real Self-content, the real meaning of life, that which makes everything meaningful. Knowing 'It' or 'Him' as himself, he finds himself free of all sorrows.

यदा पश्यः पश्यते रूक्मवर्णं कर्तारमीशं पुरूषं ब्रह्मयोनिम् ।
तदा विद्वान् पुण्यपापे विधूय निरञ्जनः परमं साम्यमुपैति ।। ३ ।।

yadā paśyaḥ paśyate rukma-varṇaṁ
kartāram īśam puruṣaṁ brahma-yonim

tadā vidvān-puṇya-pāpe vidhūya
nirañjanaḥ paramaṁ sāmyam upaiti ॥ 3 ॥

Visualizing the *Puruṣa*, the golden-hued all-doer,
All controller, source-of-Brahmā (the Creator), the wise one
Shakes off both sin and merit, and thus,
Blemishless, attains supreme Sameness.

The *Puruṣa* referred to here is the Imperishable (*akṣara*) one, the perishable (*kṣara*) one watching Him. The all-witnessing Consciousness, Effulgence, is perceived as golden-hued (*rukma-varṇam*) when considering Its value in life.

This witnessing Consciousness, when perceived in oneself, turns out to be witnessing not only oneself but everything in all the worlds. What throbs in each of us as perceiving and apperceiving is the unbounded creativity of that one *Puruṣa*. Every action that takes place anywhere in any of the worlds is but part of the self-unfoldment of the one creative urge of this one Consciousness. Realizing this one dares not think of oneself as the doer (*kartā*) of any action. The all-witnessing *Puruṣa*, the all-controller (*Īśa*), is the one doer (*kartā*) of all actions. Having no sense of agency in actions on His part, He cannot, in the sense we consider ourselves as doers, be called the doer (*kartā*) either.

Ignorant as we are of this basic fact, we attribute the responsibility for actions that take place in and through us as ours and make our life miserable with the attachments that develop and persist in connection with them and their fruits. Captives of our own ignorance, we are in search of freedom, and the only way to it is via wisdom — the awareness that what exists is the one and only Reality which is called *Puruṣa* here — and that all actions (*karmas*) are done by that *Purusa*. He is to be realized but as the witnessing Consciousness in oneself.

Indian mythology holds *Brahmā* as the Creator of the world. This concept arises from the basic notion — caused by ignorance — that the world and its creator are separately existing realities, whereas what the Upaniṣad teaches is that all that exists is one *Puruṣa* alone. What assumes the forms of these seemingly separate realities — which are mere appearances — and who perceives them as though they are distinct is the one *Puruṣa*, the one Reality, the one witnessing

Consciousness. This one *Puruṣa* himself is thus the cause of the creation of the world also.

Vidvān

The epithet *vidvān* applied to the one who knows this *Puruṣa* and rendered here as 'the wise one', means the one who is endowed with these qualities: keeping the people around contented (*jana-rañjana*), having profound thought (*gambhīrāśayatva*), honest and pleasing speech (*sad-vākyam*), a thorough reasoning faculty (*ūhāpoha-śakti*), prudence (*nayam*), wisdom (*jñānam*), propriety (*aucityam*), conformity of words and deeds, humility (*vinaya*) and firmness of conviction (*niścaya-buddhi*). All these noble qualities, in their true sense, are normally present only in the fully enlightened of the one *Puruṣa*. Being forced to commit sin, though inadvertently, is the gravest of all problems as the one involved in actions considers himself to be the real doer. So it is a matter of great concern to him. The conscientious take care to avoid sinful actions and to do propitiatory actions for the ones already committed. Given that the real doer of actions, as the Upaniṣad teaches, is the one *Puruṣa* or God and not any individual, this wisdom — knowing the *Puruṣa* as oneself — frees one from both sin and merit. Almost all religions try to help man to save himself from sin and to acquire merits; the wisdom of the Upaniṣads, on the other hand, helps man free himself from both sin and merit that cling to him and to go beyond in total freedom.

All blemishes attributed to man and his character are artefacts of social customs and concepts, all forming part of the apparent aspect of what exists and not of the one underlying Reality. The individual — the *kṣara-puruṣa*, the subject of all blemishes — seeing himself one with the *akṣara-puruṣa* finds himself free from all blemishes also. Caring only for the one Reality and not about the world's opinion, he feels free of all obligations and liabilities; the only liability he feels would be to the Absolute, which would be unlimited also.

Sāmya

A state of sameness (*sāmya*) treats both pleasures and pains, success and failure, gain and loss, with equanimity as the *Bhagavad Gītā* describes it in its Verse II.38 and elsewhere, as if elucidating the word *sāmyam* of this verse. Translatable as equality, equanimity, sameness, indifference, impartiality and so on though this word is, all its connotations derive from a wholeness (*sama*), always denoting the Absolute. The states of the two birds cited in the last verse are also integrally related to this sameness. The one who is in the state of sameness feels himself to be the controller (*īśa*) of himself as well as of everything. The other, the enjoyer, feeling that he is not the controller even of himself, watches the other and makes him his sole model. It makes him feel the same sameness while not leaving the life-tree. He thus becomes the ideal *yogī* of the *Bhagavad Gītā*. All his activities (*karmas*), including that of eating berries, get sublimated as *karma-yoga*. He sees his oneness with the life-tree, his actions merely part of the creativity of the tree and not his own.

प्राणो ह्येष यः सर्वभूतैर्विभाति विजानन् विद्वान् भवते नातिवादी ।
आत्मक्रीड आत्मरतिः क्रियावानेष ब्रह्मविदां वरिष्ठः ।। ४ ।।

prāṇo hyeṣa yaḥ sarvabhūtair-vibhāti
vijānan vidvān bhavate nātivādī ।
ātma-krīḍa ātma-ratiḥ kriyāvān
eṣa brahma-vidāṁ variṣṭhaḥ ।। 4 ।।

Truly It is the one that shines out as and through
everything;
It is the one *prāṇa* in everything.
The wise one, seeing It in all specific manifestations,
Remains reticent.
Sporting in the Self, all his actions having become
The Self 's delighting in the Self,
He is the greatest of all *Brahman*-knowers.

Anything that has emerged is a *bhūta*, and thus anything and everything in this world being a *bhūta*, it is rendered simply as 'everything' here. Such emerged entities are regarded as living and non-living ones in the popular sense, though modern science proves that there is nothing whatsoever in all the worlds that has no element of life in it.Thus life (*prāṇa*) exists not merely in what we consider as living beings (*prāṇins*). Every entity is a living entity; the cosmos as a whole is a living entity. What assumes the form of all these, and what functions as life (*prāṇa*) in all of them, is none other than the one Imperishable *Puruṣa*. Though deriving from one source, every entity is an individual, each having its own individuating characteristics, all adding up to the wholeness of the eternal flux of life. The one *Puruṣa* who becomes and keeps it thus is the *prāṇa* of all *prāṇas* (*prāṇasya prāṇaḥ*), as the *Kena Upaniṣad* prefers to put it (Verse 2). A perusal of our comments on that Upaniṣad may be helpful in this context.

Vijānan

Understood usually as the life-principle in all living beings though, the *prāṇa* as treated here shines as and through all that has emerged, as denoted by the usage *sarva-bhūtaiḥ*, not *sarva-bhūteṣu* (in all beings). This shows that everything that has emerged, the vital principle in them all, the consciousness that systematizes the whole, are all various apparent forms assumed by the one *Puruṣa*. Knowing this *Puruṣa*, therefore, means realising Him as the one Reality that underlies all the apparent specific forms, as is implicit in the word *vijānan*, *vi* standing for specific forms (*viśeṣa*) and *jānan* for one who knows.

Reticent

The experience of the one anchored in and embedded in *Brahman*, as an arrow in its target, being what is enunciated in these verses, it is not something to be demonstrated to anyone else. Nor is it to be proved to a gathering of experts. The one of this experience simply remains wordless in the blissfulness of the transcendental sameness (*sāmyatā*) where all argumentation becomes meaningless. It might be that he will share his blissfulness with someone who approaches him in all earnestness, in all faith; then too what he has to finally reveal will necessarily be clothed in a silence brimming with a rich meaningfulness. Where no word avails, of what avail will any argument be? He simply remains reticent, even if it so happens that the whole world runs him down.

Brahmavidām-variṣṭhaḥ

Brahman, the Imperishable *Puruṣa*, is realized by the seeker, not as an object, but as the Substance of his own being, and therefore, it could from now on be called *ātmā* or *ātman*, the Self. Whatever till then was felt to be the cause of one's suffering, now turns out to be but part of the sport of that one *ātman*. All life thus is realized as nothing more than a drama enacted by the Self in the stage of the Self, for the Self.

This sporting of the Self is a creative one. Nothing in all the worlds is outside its arena. My own existence, my activities, both physical and mental, are all merely part of the manoeuvring of this sporting, or mere momentary sparkings of the great bonfire of the creative self-expression of the Self-Reality.

All sport involvement is intended to arouse joy. The great sport of the Self in the Self is no exception, its joy being that of uncovering the *ānanda* (happiness) content of the Self to Itself. One who thus sees himself and all the worlds and their ever-changing phenomenal appearances, as part of the Self's sport, and not existing apart from It, is the greatest of all *Brahman*-knowers (*brahmavid-variṣṭhaḥ*).

Up till now in this section we have been discriminating between the perishable (*kṣara*) and Imperishable (*akṣara*) *puruṣa*s in terms of an experiential awareness, vivifying meanwhile the experience of attaining the Imperishable *Puruṣa*. The way one attains this goal and becomes a *vidvān* (a wise one), is indicated in the next verse, again in the tone of an intuitive experience, where the emphasis is on the method of attaining rather than on what is attained.

सत्येन लभ्यस्तपसा ह्येष आत्मा सम्यग्ज्ञानेन ब्रह्मचर्येण नित्यम् ।
अन्तःशरीरे ज्योतिर्मयो हि शुभ्रो यं पश्यन्ति यतयः क्षीणदोषाः ॥ ५ ॥

satyena labhyas tapasā hy eṣa ātmā
samyag-jñānena brahmacaryeṇa nityam ।
antaḥ śarīre jyotirmayo hi śubraḥ
yaṁ paśyanti yatayaḥ kṣīṇa-doṣāḥ ॥ 5 ॥

Obtainable through Truth (*satya*) and *tapas* is that *ātmā*,
As also through proper knowledge (*jñāna*) and proper
studentship constantly practised;

Within the perishable appearance (*śarīra*) is that *ātmā*,
effulgence in essence, the Pure,
Perceived by those of self-restraint and weakened blemishes.

Unlike gaining an object, for example, a precious gem, the gaining of the Self signified here is the seeker's experiencing his oneness with what he seeks, like the state of an arrow piercing its target. Or it could be likened to the state of a drop of clear water that falls into an ocean of clear water, which, in fact, is not a gain at all. In a state in which the gainer is lost in what is gained, there will be nothing 'to gain' as such, or rather it is an experience of having gained everything gainable.

Gaining the Self, we have already seen, is to be accomplished by making oneself the arrow aimed at *Brahman*, the target. Oneself, the arrow is real; *Brahman*, the target, is real; *praṇava*, the bow, is real. The process, thus, is one in which the Real attains the Real with the instrumentality of the Real. The usage 'obtainable through Truth' (*satyena labhyaḥ*) thus signifies a very broad and intuitive perspective.

The significance of *tapas*, a self-imposed self-heating discipline, has been examined under Verse I.ii.11. Undergone by self in order to know itself, it is a discipline — indeed the only discipline — where ends becomes means and *vice versa*.

The knowing subject in this knowledge is the Self and the known object is also the very same Self. The duality of subject and object as well as that of ends and means, thus vanishes in Self-knowledge. It is where knowledge attains its finality, denoted by the word *samyag-jñānena* (through proper knowledge).

Brahmacarya

Not a mere theoretical understanding, the wisdom of the Absolute (*brahma-jñāna*) is a way of life — living as *Brahman*. Making *Brahman*-knowledge one's way of life is what is signified by the word *brahma-carya*, *carya* meaning way of living, though celebacy is generally considered to be denoted by it. Mere celebacy does not make one a *brahma-cārin*, nor does leading a married life necessarily make one a non-*brahma-cārin*. Celebacy admittedly becomes natural with most of those who are fully dedicatedly to *Brahman*. The traditional name for proper studentship, a stage in life when normally one is unmarried, is also *brahma-carya*. What is of import in a *brahma-cārin*'s life is the viewing of all life as a sport of *ātman* or *Brahman*. Having such a vision of life is not merely to be uncovered at certain moments as when meditating. Every moment in one's life, on the other hand, needs to be a forward step in the path of *brahmacarya*, as is indicated by the word *nityam* (constantly practised).

Antaḥ-śarīre

Though commonly interpreted as 'body' the word *śarīra* literally means 'that which perishes', and *antaḥ-śarīra* means 'within that which perishes', rendered here as 'within the perishable appearance'. *Śarīra* in the Vedāntic context, equated to *kṣetra* (field) by the *Bhagavad Gītā* (XIII.1), includes everything that perishes, even the animating principle in an organism not exempted, as confirmed in Verse XIII.6-7 of the *Gītā*.* Compelled by the unconscious preconditioning of our minds, we might be misled by the word *antaḥ* (within) of the present verse, to think of *ātmā* as seated at some particular point or hollow within the body. Unlike the 'within' in water within a container, it is like the gold within ornaments, water within waves. Construing the Self as seated at any particular point only annuls its own oneness and all-pervasiveness.

Jyotir-maya (effulgence in essence) means the same as the word (*divya*) of Verse II.i.2, and *arcimat* of II.ii.2, whose implications we have already examined. *Śubhra* (the Pure) of the verse and *nirañjana* (the blemishless) of Verse III.i.3 above mean the same.

Blemishes Weakened

Aware though we are of what is deficient in us, what is wrong in us, our pattern of behaviour with others is the only measuring rod that helps us decide our rights and wrongs. Once there is no one 'else ', no 'other',

---

* The great elements, I-sense, reason, and also the unmanifest, the ten senses, the mind, the five sense-objects, wish, dislike, pleasure-pain, the organic aggregates, the vital principle (*cetanā*), fortitude: all these in brief form the *kṣetra*, said to be changeful. (*Bhagavad Gītā*, XIII.6-7)

to deal with, the question of rightness and wrongness of our behaviour becomes meaningless. A *jñānin* is a person who sees everything as a sporting of the Self — of Himself — not existing apart from the Self. He thus sees nothing as 'other' than himself, and by the same token is free from all rights and wrongs in behaviour. Self-knowledge and absolution from blemishes thus always go together, one meaningless without the other: the implication of the word *kṣīṇa-doṣāḥ* (of weakened blemishes).

सत्यमेव जयते नानृतं सत्येन पन्था विततो देवयानः ।
येनाक्रमन्त्यृषयो ह्याप्तकामा यत्र तत् सत्यस्य परमं निधानम् ॥ ६ ॥

satyam eva jayate nānṛtaṁ
satyena panthā vitato devayānaḥ ।
yena ākramanti ṛṣayo hyāptakāmā
yatra tat satyasya paramaṁ nidhānam ॥ 6 ॥

Truth alone succeeds; not untruth.
By Truth is laid out the path of gods,
The path through which the seers with fulfilled desires
Cross over to where exists the supreme repository of that very same Truth.

That *ātmā* alone exists, *ātmā* alone manifesting as everything, has been laid bare in the preceding verses. What appears thus as all the changeful worlds is the creative advance, the success, of the Self — an advance involving the downfall of nothing. Seeing one's own life as part of this creative advance of the Self — the Truth — one finds one's thoughts, words and deeds to have already fallen fully in line with that Truth. The prevailing of Truth will then be evident in one's personal life as well. Do practise to hold on to Truth in thought, words and deeds every moment in life. Though this may feel a bit difficult at first, success eventually ensues — the success of having gained a constantly felt peace of mind, as though it is God's bounty.

Anṛta

Ṛta means the overall system of life as the spontaneous unfolding of what is Real; *anṛta*, its opposite, means that which is in discord with that system. Our emergence and living are a part of *ṛta* — the advance, the success, of the Self-Reality. Yet we, in our ignorance, unmindful of *ṛta,* try to create a world of our own, to make a life system of our own, mindful only of our personal interests. As long as such attempts are fully in tune with the scheme of the unfoldment of the total life, peace prevails in life; to the extent that they clash with that scheme untruth (*anṛta*) prevails, rendering life restless and turbulent. Appearing like success in the beginning, it ends up as a big failure, suffused with sufferings.

Devayāna

Devayāna, meaning the path of gods, stands here for the way of wisdom and Truth, as the literal sense of the word *deva*, that which is effulgence in essence, suggests. The word, as Vedic ritualism conceives it, refers to one of the two paths the departed souls pass through — *devayāna* by the souls of the wise — past the brightness of fire, day-time, the brighter fortnight, the brighter half-year, eventually reaching the world of *Brahman*, never to return to this world; through the other path — *pitṛyāna*, the path of manes — pass departed souls of the ignorant, past dark smoke, night, the darker fortnight, the darker half-year and so on, ending up in the *pitṛloka* (the world of manes), eventually to return to this world again when the merits previously acquired get exhausted. Vedānta, a revaluation of Vedism and its concepts, instead of doing away with such concepts, adopts them into its body, adapting them to the wisdom context. *Devayāna* is the concept so revalued here as the path of effulgence or wisdom.

Wisdom's way of life is thus laid out wide before us by the Truth, the very goal it aims at. What is required of us is to see it and adapt to it with a firm mind.

With Fulfilled Desires

Jumping into that path and treading along it is no easy task. Only those endowed with a resolute mind and a transparent vision of the goal to be attained and the means to be adopted, would willingly jump onto it. Those of such vision — called here *ṛṣayaḥ* or seers — interested as they are in the one goal this path leads to, feel all other desires to be of no significance. Once the goal is reached, they are real *ṛṣi*s (seers), an achievement that gives the satisfaction of having fulfilled all desires. Considering pleasure-seeking as the goal of life, on the other hand, makes life an endless chase for enjoyable objects, where satisfying one desire leads to another in an endless succession, finally reaching nowhere. Those who live under the spell of such desires are known as *kāma-hata*s (lost themselves in desires). All such desires get obliterated, as stars in broad daylight, on one's finding *Brahman*, the Truth. Having crossed over to Its supreme repository, by knowing what is real in oneself, one finds oneself well founded in that Truth, oneself to be that Truth, everything to be nothing but that Truth — the Truth that is the repository of all the worlds (*paramam nidhānam*).

बृहच्च तद् दिव्यमचिन्त्यरूपं सूक्ष्माच्च तत् सूक्ष्मतरं विभाति ।
दूरात् सुदूरे तदिहान्तिके च पश्यत्स्विहैव निहितं गुहायाम् ।। ७।।

bṛhac ca tad divyam acintya-rūpaṁ
sūkṣmāc ca tat sūkṣma-taraṁ vibhāti ।
dūrāt sudūre tad ihāntike ca
paśyatsv ihaiva nihitaṁ guhāyām ।। 7 ।।

The far-extended, the self-effulgent,
Of inconceivable form, minuter than the minutest,
It becomes visible as all.
Farther away from the farthest,
Yet here near at hand,
It is perceived by those who perceive intuitively,
As remaining here itself as if in a secret abode.

The paradoxes seekers would have to encounter as they set off in search of *Brahman* are what this verse lays bare.

Meaning that which is extensive (*bṛhat*), the word *Brahman* stands for the Reality that is always in the process of limitless growth. Pure Consciousness, It is effulgence in essence (*divya*). Nothing other than consciousness reaches out to limitlessness.

Thinking, a particular functional mode of consciousness, helps us conceive ideas. Yet, making its own source its object of thinking is something unthinkable, like an eye being unable to see itself; and thus *Brahman* always remains inconceivable.

Everything experienced is categorizable either as gross or subtle. A tangible object is gross; beauty is a subtle experience. Even the supposedly gross elements of nature — earth, water, fire, air, space — are referred to in the order of their subtlety or grossness: the earth the grossest and space the subtlest. Viewed thus, when we attempt to conceive of *Brahman*, It can be thought of only as the subtlest of all, or as minuter than the minutest — while at the same time the most extensive, bringing about thus a paradoxical situation; all a fallout of our attempt to conceive of *Brahman*. Minuteness and extensiveness, both are mere ideas that become manifest as two functional modes of the one Consciousness — *Brahman* — as is suggested by the word *vibhāti* (becomes visible apparent as). Beyond all measure, *Brahman* as such is neither minute nor extensive.

Once experienced as the essential content of one's own being — the only way of knowing *Brahman* — It is felt as the nearest of all realities, as an ornament feels gold to be nearest to it. The real philosopher, as Vedānta maintains, the real seer, is the one who intuitively perceives Reality thus as one's own beingness, as oneself inseparably one with It. Though our most direct experience, it cannot be shown to someone else. How the other can and is to know It, is as his or her own beingness. Though evident to the transparancy of the intent seeker's intuitive perception, It always remains invisible in the ordinary sense of visibility, one may even consider It as always hidden in an unreachable hideout (*guha*).

न चक्षुषा गृह्यते नापि वाचा नान्यैर्देवैस्तपसा कर्मणा वा ।
ज्ञानप्रसादेन विशुद्धसत्त्वस्ततस्तु तं पश्यते निष्कलं ध्यायमानः ॥ ८ ॥

na cakṣuṣā gṛhyate nāpi vācā
nānyair devais tapasā karmaṇā vā ।
jñāna-prasādena viśuddha-sattvaḥ
tatas tu taṁ paśyate niṣkalaṁ dhyāyamānaḥ ॥ 8 ॥

Not by the eyes is It grasped, nor even by speech!
Not by other sense organs, *tapas* or *karma*;
Beyond all this, however,
Purified in mind by the graciousness of wisdom,
One meditating, intuitively perceives It, the partless.

With the eyes we perceive forms and colours; yet the Consciousness, the Reality, that unfolds itself as the eyes, as sight, and as the forms and colours seen, all together forming an ensemble, never becomes an object for eyes to see. So too the Consciousness that gets transformed as ideas, that coins words and imbues them with ideas as their meanings, thus making communication possible, can never be bottled up in any word as its meaning. The same applies to all the sense organs and organs of action — the eyes represent the former and speech the latter.

Having already stated in Verse I.ii.11 that *tapas* is the most helpful way to reach the abode of the Immortal *Puruṣa*, the present statement that *Brahman* is ungraspable even by undergoing *tapas*, may sound strange. The previous reference to *tapas* was as a help to the seeker to reach his goal, like an arrow reaching its target and becoming well-fixed there — not a state of grasping the goal as though it were an object. What is denied in this present verse is this latter aspect. The only way of realizing *Brahman* being as one's own self-content. It is ungraspable as an object even to those who undergo *tapas*. Anyone's claim, if made after a prolonged *tapas*, to know *Brahman*, should not therefore be taken as a genuine one; a genuine *Brahman*-knower can make no such claim, one of the basic tenets of all the Upaniṣads. The *Kena Upaniṣad*, for example, emphatically says:

To the one who does not know It, is It known;
And unknown is It to the one who knows It.
(Verse 12)

Karmas (actions), whether ritualistic or otherwise, are always benifit-motivated. The attaining of *Brahman* being not the result of any action, It is unattainable through *karmas*.

Jñāna (wisdom) is the experience of one's having reached the goal, having become one with it, and having realized that oneself as well as everything else has no existence apart from that. Seeing oneself as one with *Brahman*, all that happens in one's life gets transformed as aspects of the unfolding of that *Brahman*; all problems and miseries also thus melt down into the existence of *Brahman*, in the unfolding of *Brahman*. Free of all blemishes, of all miseries, of all problems, one experiences one's life simply as the graciousness of *Brahman*. This experience is attained in meditaion — a meditation into which the practitioner's life — progress gets transformed, not a meditation practised merely for a few minutes, or even hours, in a closed room or a secluded place. Life and meditation are inseparably one for them. The attainment of wisdom, its graciousness, purity of mind, meditation, the intuitive perception of *Brahman*, all these thus do not occur in sequence. Simultaneous experiences as they are, they are merely various experiential facets of the one and only non-duality.

एषोऽणुरात्मा चेतसा वेदितव्यो यस्मिन् प्राणः पञ्चधा संविवेश ।
प्राणैश्चित्तं सर्वमोतं प्रजानां यस्मिन् विशुद्धे विभवत्येष आत्मा ॥ ९ ॥

eṣoṇurātmā cetasā veditavyo
yasmin prāṇaḥ pañcadhā saṁviveśa ।
praṇaiś cittaṁ sarvam otaṁ prajānāṁ
yasmin viśuddhe vibhavaty eṣa ātmā ॥ 9 ॥

Realizable is this subtlest Self
As the Consciousness into which
Are infused the five-fold *prāṇa*s.
Woven into by the five-fold *prāṇa*s
Is this functional Consciousness (*citta*) of all born beings!
To that consciousness, when blemishless, is this Self self-revealed.

The uncontaminated state of consciousness (*śuddha-sattva*), considered in the last verse as that wherein the self gets revealed to oneself, is what is elaborated on in this verse.

Cetas is the awareness of self-existence each living being has. *Cetas* as such, in its uncontaminated state, becoming revealed to one is not commonplace; infused with the five *prāṇa*s as it always is, its state is known as *cetana*. When the thinking faculty — in whose presence alone one reflects on oneself as well as everything else — is added, *cetana* becomes *citta*. Reflecting mind (*citta*) thus has *cetana* behind it, energizing it to reflect, and this *cetana* in its turn is inter-woven by the five-fold *prāṇa*s. The reflecting faculty left behind, *citta* becomes purified as *cetana*; the *prāṇa*s not involved, *cetana* becomes purified as *cetas* — the pure mind (*viśuddha-sattva*), wherein the seeker, through meditation, perceives his own real self-content. Or rather, that uncontaminated mind, the unconditioned state of Consciousness, is itself the real self-content of oneself, the Self.

यं यं लोकं मनसा संविभाति विशुद्धसत्त्वः कामयते यांश्च कामान् ।
तं तं लोकं जयते तांश्च कामांस्तस्मादात्मज्ञं ह्यर्चयेत् भूतिकामः ॥ १० ॥

yaṁ yaṁ lokaṁ manasā saṁvibhāti
viśuddha-sattvaḥ kāmayate yāṁśca kāmān ।
taṁ taṁ lokaṁ jayate tāṁśca kāmān
tasmād-ātmajñaṁ hyarcayet bhūtikāmaḥ ॥ 10 ॥

Whichever the world the purified-in-mind
Perceives clearly in his mind,
Whichever the desire that arises in him,
(as Self's unfoldment),
Those worlds he wins over, those desires as well;
Those desirous of welfare, therefore
Should adore the Self-knowers.

Who the purified-in-mind is — himself the self-knower — having been made clear, this verse proceeds to show why he is to adored and how.

The word *jayate*, rendered here as 'wins over', being in fact interpretable as 'attains' as well as 'restrains', the verse as well is construable in two ways.

In the former sense, whatever the worlds he perceives, externally or internally, as Self's spontaneous unfoldment, he attains them in the very same way. His mind and the world being not two in essence, what he perceives as the world is what he imagines; what he imagines is what he perceives as the world. Likewise, whatever be the desire that arises in his mind, as part of the unfoldment of the Self, it gets fulfilled as a natural process of life, with no intentional effort on his part.

In the latter sense, on the other hand, whatever the concepts and images be that arise in his mind, he restrains himself from their temptations. Whenever desires arise in his mind, he controls them and triumphs over them.

Indifference to the projected worlds as an essential prerequisite for a seeker of *Brahman*, and as natural to a *Brahman*-knower having been emphasized in Verse I.ii.12, and that the *Brahman*-knower perceives one *Brahman* alone as pervading all the worlds — before, behind, to the right, to the left, above, below — having been made explicit in Verse II.ii.11, it would be meaningless to conceive of a *Brahman*-knower thinking of some other desirable world or worlds or even feeling some desires yet unfulfilled. He remains always fully satisfied that he has attained all the attinable worlds, of having no unfulfilled desires, as he sees all the other worlds, all the desirable objects, as not existing apart from him. Such is the peculiar way he attains other worlds.

The same applies to his desires. That only those who feel a sense of detachment from desirables are capable of entering the sacred realm of wisdom has already been made sufficiently clear; and the beginning of the next section also claims that 'the desireless' (*akāmaḥ*) alone attain the ultimate goal and leave behind the causal seed of birth and death. Given all these, it would be pointless to state that all the desires of the *Brahman*-knower would get fulfilled in the ordinary sense. His satisfaction in having no unfulfilled desires, on the other hand, is in having no desire at all.

Those who are desirous of well-being in life, it is advised, should adore the knower of the Self; not that adoring holy men is the best way to acquire worldly gains. Misled by such scriptural pronouncements are the rich people who do services and perform *pūjā*s to holy men with the unholy intention of gaining more wealth. The knowers of the Self are desireless; they have gone beyond or overcome all desires. To think of gaining what they themselves consider as repugnant, by doing service to them and by adoring them is nonsense. What could be gained thus is but what they themselves cherish. What they cherish is gained by those adore them as well. Worldly prosperity, therefore, is not at all the intention of the *bhūtikāma*s (those desirous of welfare) of this verse. What kind of well-being it is is clearly stated in the next verse with which the next section begins: the contentment of knowing the world in its purity and of leaving the causal seed of birth and death behind.

Khaṇḍa 2

The first four verses of this section form an elucidation on the statement with which the last section concluded : that those who are desirous of well-being in life should adore the knowers of the Self. The rest of the section is by way of concluding the Upaniṣad pointing at the ultimate benefit of its study.

स वेदैतत् परमं ब्रह्म धाम यत्र विश्वं निहितं भाति शुभ्रम् ।
उपासते पुरूषं ये ह्यकामास्ते शुक्रमेतदतिवर्तन्ति धीराः ।। १ ।।

sa vedaitat paramaṁ brahma dhāma
yatra viśvaṁ nihitaṁ bhāti śubhram ।
upāsate puruṣaṁ ye hyakāmāḥ
te śukram etad-ativartanti dhīrāḥ ।। 1 ।।

Founded wherein this world shines in its purity,
That Supreme abode, *Brahman,* is known to him.
Those desireless who adore that person,
Wise and firm-in-mind, they leave behind the seed of birth.

That the Imperishable *Puruṣa*, the abode of all the worlds, is none other than *ātmā*, the Self, was made sufficiently clear in *Muṇḍaka* II which ended with the words: "By Its light it is that everything specifically shines." The entire speculation developed in that *Muṇḍaka* has been summarized and put in a nutshell in the first half of this Verse. The 'him' (*saḥ*) referred to in this verse is the *bhūtikāmaḥ* (the one desirous of well-being) of the last verse. That what he gains is not any worldly prosperity is evident. The ideal *bhūtikāma*s are really desireless (*akāmāḥ*) and what they gain by adoring the knowers of the Self is revealed in the second half of the verse.

The *Puruṣa* of this verse could be taken as the person who knows the Self, or the Imperishable *Puruṣa*, the Reality that permeates as its essence the entire text of this Upaniṣad. The person who knows the Self — the *Brahman*-knower — and the all-pervading *Puruṣa* are not basically two, as the knower of *Brahman* finds himself existing in *Brahman*, as *Brahman*: the final attainment of a *jñānin* as upheld by the famous Upaniṣadic pronouncement, "The *Brahman*-knower is *Brahman* indeed" (*brahma-veda brahmaiva bhavati*), appearing in Verse 9 of this very section. The two *puruṣa*s thus need to be considered one by us as well as by the one who adores the *Puruṣa*.

Liberation (*mukti*) from all bondages is the ultimate goal of all Vedāntic enquiry including liberation from the repeated life-cycles of birth and death. The cause of life-cycles or *saṁsāra*, figuratively conceived here as *śukram* (semen), is therefore to be left behind. This is to be accomplished, this verse suggests, by those who do *upāsanā* (sitting down nearby and doing services) to the knowers of the Self. The attainment of well-being cited earlier is none other than this Liberation. *Upāsanā* stands, therefore, for the intimacy one needs to establish with *Brahman* as well as with the knower of *Brahman*, achievable only by *dhīrāḥ* (those who are endowed with a firmness of mind attained through having and imparting wisdom).

कामान् यः कामयते मन्यमानः स कामभिर्जायते तत्र तत्र ।
पर्याप्तकामस्य कृतात्मनस्तु इहैव सर्वे प्रविलीयन्ति कामाः ।। २ ।।

kāmān yaḥ kāmayate manyamānaḥ
sa kāmabhir jāyate tatra tatra ।
paryāpta-kāmasya kṛtāmanas tu
ihaiva sarve pravilīyanti kāmāḥ ।। 2 ।।

Resolutely desiring the enjoyables,
One is born again in accordance with one's desires
Accompanied by the very desires.
With the one of fulfilled desires, on the other hand,

Himself transformed as the Self,
All his desires die out here and now.

What one considers as of highest value decides the nature of one's thoughts, words and deeds in life. No thinking will take those who consider worldly prosperity to be what makes life meaningful out of the bonds of worldly concerns. Their thinking helps only to strengthen their resoluteness to strive for more worldly gains. What one gains is in accordance with what one desires. It may be that all the expectations are not fulfilled, yet one never in such cases attains more than one has estimated possible. With the desire to attain the Absolute the final goal Upaniṣadic wisdom aims at, this is not so. What one attains there is always beyond what one anticipates, as the Absolute is beyond all calculations. The one who is interested in the Absolute becomes one with the Absolute; one interested in worldly gains becomes one with them. What one is interested in thus determines the essentials of the individuality of a person. The following words of the *Bhagavad Gītā* (XVII.3) could be considered as an outpouring of this psychological secret:

Man is made up of what he has faith in:
Of what faith a man is, that, indeed, he is.

That performance of all desire-based actions pertains to *aparā-vidyā* (immanent knowledge) having been seen at the beginning of the Upaniṣad, and a detailed description of the happiness that results from such actions and the worlds reached by their performers having been given in Verses 5 to 10 of Section 2 of the first *Muṇḍaka*, the first half of the present verse could well be considered a summary of it. The *paryāpta-kāma* (one of fulfilled desires) is none other than the *āpta-kāma* of Verse III.i.6. *Kṛtātmā*, a new expression that appears in this verse, is the name given to the one described all through the second *Muṇḍaka*. A *kṛtātmā* (one transformed as the Self), with no personal desires, sees no unattained desirables. He constantly feels the contentment of having fulfilled all desires, and thus he is a *paryāpta-kāma*.

Those under the spell of desires, whether they adore knowers of the Self or not, gain what they desire — worldly joys. For the one of fulfilled desires, on the other hand, the attainment of his goal — Self-realization — solely depends on his approaching a real knower of the Self and adoring him. The *bhūtikāma* (those desirous of well-being), mentioned in the concluding verse of the last section, therefore, must be none other than the *paryāpta-kāma* of the present verse.

नायमात्मा प्रवचनेन लभ्यो न मेधया न बहुना श्रुतेन ।
यमेवैष वृणुते तेन लभ्यस्तस्यैष आत्मा विवृणुते तनुं स्वाम् ।। ३ ।।

nāyam ātmā pravacanena labhyo
na medhyā na bahunā śrutena ।
yam evaiṣa vṛṇute tena labhyaḥ
tasyaiṣa ātmā vivṛṇute tanuṁ svām ।। 3 ।।

This (Self) is unattainable by instruction;
Nor by intellectual power, nor even by much learning of scriptures.
One chooses It (the Self) alone as such,
And thus alone is It attainable.
To him the Self unveils Itself.

Verbatim repeated in the *Kaṭha Upaniṣad* (I.ii.23), the present unique verse exposes the uniqueness of wisdom teaching *vis-a-vis* the attainment of the Self. Listening to instructions and discourses (*pravacana*) given by scholars, reading scriptures and other spiritual texts along with their elucidations, using one's own intellectual acumen, are all means resorted to by those who are interested in spiritual matters. Yet Self-realization, the ultimate goal of all such enquirers, this verse underlines, remains unattainable by any or all such means.

Those who listen to and give excellent and interesting discourses on spiritual matters are many. Those who write interesting and scholarly books, even with original insight, on such matters are also legion. Many spend a lot of time trying to unravel the intricacies of spiritual texts. All of them, however, live just like anyone else, engrossed in and inflicted by the trials and tribulations of worldly life. The wisdom they try to understand and teach in no way transforms them into real *jñānins* (the wise ones) or self-realized persons. Had it been so, how many Self-realized persons would there have been in this world! Such peoples' number would have grown in proportion to the copies of sold-out spiritual books! Nothing of this kind happens. The real Self-realized person is rare indeed, in spite of all the learned discourses listened to and popular books sold and read. Clearing the path to the goal though they are, the actual attainment of the goal is of a quite different order from that which such practices lead to.

Those who aspire to well-being in life (*bhūtikāmas*), after discriminating between what is of value and what is of no value, choose to own nothing but the Self—their own Self—and stand firmly by that. To them alone is attainable the final goal—the Self—deigned by the wisdom teaching of this Upaniṣad.

How this realization is actualized is also disclosed here. The gaining of the Self is unlike the gaining of anything else. Already oneself, the Self remains veiled in the seeker as his own beingness. To the one who chooses that veiled Self alone as of any value does the Self unveil Itself, comparable to a bride's disclosing her whole body (*tanu*) to the one who, excluding all others, chooses her alone to be his. So too the seekers forgo their external duality and merge in one beingness. The one who chooses the Self also forgoes all conditioning factors and finds his beingness in the beingness of the one Reality, the Absolute Self (*paramātman*). It is thus that the Self-Reality gets self-revealed, where the duality between the seeker and the sought merge in the unitiveness of One Beingness.

नायमात्मा बलहीनेन लभ्यो न च प्रमादात् तपसो वाप्यलिङ्गात् ।
एतैरुपायैर्यतते यस्तु विद्वांस्तस्यैष आत्मा विशते ब्रह्मधाम ॥ ४॥

nāyam ātmā balahīnena labhyo
na ca pramādāt tapaso vāpy aliṅgāt ।
etair upayair yatate yastu vidvāms
tasyaiṣa ātmā viśate brahmadhāma ॥ 4 ॥

This Self is not to be obtained by one destitute of

fortitude;
Nor is It obtainable to the heedless;
Neither through austerity devoid of external signs.
Yet the one who strives by these means,
Provided he is a learned and intent seeker,
He finds himself (the Self) already in the *Brahman*-abode.

Essential for the attainment of the Self, fortitude implies physical strength also. Strength, in fact, is never of body or mind separately, but of the person as a whole, body and mind being only two apparent aspects of the individual being. To consider obtaining the Self as the sole goal of life and to forgo all pleasures for its sake, needs much strength. A weakling never succeeds in this.

Heedful effort on the part of the seeker is essential for the attainment of this goal. To be fully convinced that the Self is the sole meaning of life and attaining it the sole gole of life, is not enough by itself. One has also to be constantly on the alert against infatuations and vulnerability in weak moments, even willing to suffer so that this may be so. Such heedlessness and vulnerability together is called *pramāda*. This aspect was emphasized as early as Verse II.ii.4 where it was said that the self-arrow is to be shot at the *Brahman*-target 'unerringly' (*apramattena*). No wisdom text, in fact, leaves unstressed the importance of this heedfulness that makes every moment of life a moment of trial.

The role of *tapas* (austere self-heating) is elusive indeed. That without it no Self-gaining would be possible was underscored in Verse III.i.5., but here the stress is that even *tapas* would be of no avail if devoid of its external signs (*aliṅgāt*).

Being an internal self-heating process, should *tapas* have any external manifestation in the behaviour pattern of its performer? Many are those who are familiar with the subtle intricacies of wisdom teaching and capable of elucidating them; yet the evidence of wisdom may be totally absent in their practical life. They may even claim, "I am not a person who cares for customs and practices. Wisdom is knowledge of what is Real, and I know what it is." Should such be treated as *jñānin*s and their intellectual acumen as *tapas*?

The Self, the meaning content of all life, is to be realized by the seeker as the meaning content of his own beingness — a meaning-content that lives. Life, in other words, is the visible sign of the existence of that Reality. The knowledge of the Self that does not actually get expresseed in life, therefore, cannot be true wisdom. Only that wisdom that finds expression in actual life is the living wisdom. The means of attaining that wisdom should also be a living one. *Tapas* devoid of visible signs is therefore no *tapas*; wisdom devoid of visible signs is no wisdom.

The opposites of the factors mentioned here as blocking the way to the final goal, all promote it. How *tapas* could be helpful and unhelpful has been clarified in our comments on Verses I. ii.11, III.i.5 and III.i.8. Self-effort with proper *tapas* practised in the proper way, strenghened by fortitude and awareness, is alone conducive to the proper attainment of the Self, which in effect is not an attainment at all as It is a state in which one finds oneself already in It and one with It rather than stepping into It. The seeker finds It his proper abode, which till that moment was quite unknown to him. In one's own abode alone one remains as oneself, devoid of all pretentiousness. There is loss of self-identity in the all-inclusive *Brahman* — this gaining of the Self in effect is the loss of oneself. With *Brahman* as one's abode, one unmasks one's self of all the conditioning factors of self-identity, to be lost in Its oneness, never to return to the world of multiplicity and self-identity.

संप्राप्यैनमृषयो ज्ञानतृप्ताः कृतात्मानो वीतरागाः प्रशान्ताः
ते सर्वगं सर्वतः प्राप्य धीरा युक्तात्मानः सर्वमेवाविशन्ति ॥ ५ ॥

saṁprāpya enam ṛṣayo jñāna-tṛptāḥ
kṛtātmāno vītarāgāḥ praśāntāḥ ।
te sarvagaṁ sarvataḥ prāpya dhīrā
yuktātmānaḥ sarvam eva āviśanti ॥ 5 ॥

Duly attaining *Brahman*, the seers,
Already transformed as the Self,
Free from attachments and tranquil in mind,
Become content in wisdom.

Having become one with the all-pervasive One everywhere,
They, of unitive Self-content,
Get merged with all.

The oneness of all in the Self, with its blissfulness constantly experienced by those of final attainment, is what we witness in the remaining verses of this Upaniṣad as the culmination of its teaching.

These verses need no comment. All their ideas have already appeared and been commented upon. What is required now is, by means of meditation and through the transformation of one's own life via that meditation , one must actualize the wisdom-contentment and one's oneness with all. The contentment this wisdom results in is that of having known what is the essential life-knowledge, the knowledge without which life would remain empty. Those of that contentment are to be called *jñāna-tṛpta*s.

One who sees one's self-existence as one with the existence of all, one who experiences unitiveness with the one Self, is to be called a *yuktātmā*.

That every practical life-situation is seen by such a *yuktātmā* as an instance of actualizing his oneness with the Absolute or *Brahman* or the Self, is suggested by the words *sarvagam sarvataḥ prāpya* (having become one with the all-pervasive One everywhere).

वेदान्तविज्ञानसुनिश्चितार्थाः संन्यासयोगाद् यतयः शुद्धसत्त्वाः ।
ते ब्रह्मलोकेषु परान्तकाले परामृताः परिमुच्यन्ति सर्वे ।। ६ ।।

vedānta-vijñāna-suniścitārthāḥ
saṁnyāsa-yogād yatayaḥ śuddha-sattvāḥ ।
te brahma-lokeṣu parānta-kāle
parāmṛtāḥ parimucyanti sarve ।। 6 ।।

With what Vedānta teaches having become a certitude,
Those of self-restraint, through the yoga of renunciation,
Attain pure beingness.
Absolutely Immortal as they are all,

Liberated in all respects into the *Brahman*-world
They become, as time ultimately terminates.

"What happens to us after death?" is the problem that puzzles all of us, and is the one problem that urges us on to think of the meaning of our present life. That the meaning content of the apparent phenomenon of life is one Immortal Reality which alone has an existence of its own, has become sufficiently clear as we passed through the text and comments on this Upaniṣad. Given that the Reality that underlies the phenomenon of life is birthless and deathless, the problem of the hereafter vanishes of its own accord as that Reality has to continue to exist even after what we call death. The Upaniṣad till now has been potraying how that Immortal Substance, called *Puruṣa, akṣara puruṣa, Brahman* or *ātman*, endures endlessly in and through the apparent phenomena of birth and death of individuated entities.

The theme of this Upaniṣad was one particular perspective: how the secret wisdom of *Brahman* could be attained. Such perspectives being endlessly many, each Upaniṣad adopts a chosen one. No matter what the particular perspective each Upaniṣad resorts to, the final wisdom — the certitude of the immortality of oneself, the Self, revealed in all of them, the crux that matters — remains unchanged.

An individual, a seeker, like an arrow, getting fired at the *Brahman*-target and becoming merged with and lodged in that Target, is the core of the teaching of the present Upaniṣad. To renounce (*saṁnyāsa*) oneself thus in effect in this case is the attainment of union (*yoga*) with Reality, making of it *saṁnyāsa-yoga* (the *yoga* of renunciation). Those in this state of yoga find themselves existing unconditioned by any limitations as pure beingness (*śuddha-sattva*).

The usage *brahma-lokeṣu*, literally in the *Brahman* worlds, though suggestive of plurality of such worlds indicates, according to Śaṅkara, that each individual's concept of the *Brahman*-world is most probably a different one, yet the one *Brahman*-world remains unaffected.

For those to whom the Vedānta teaching has become a certitude, the essential content of their being is one Immortal Reality, *ānanda* in essence, as already suggested in Verse II.ii-7 as *ānanda-rūpam-amṛtam*, and the same immortal Reality would and should continue to exist even after the so-called death. Death is nothing but the event of becoming free of all the conditioning that until then caused one to be an individual. The Reality, while continuing to exist, should take on new conditioning factors, as a gold ornament melted down takes on a new apparent form. The Self-Reality remains unchanged in spite of the constant changes that take place in appearance. This getting liberated from individuating conditionings is what is portrayed in the next verse.

The ultimate termination of time (*parānta-kāle*) does not necessarily stand for the event of death. The liberated one is even free of time limitations. Time is meaningful only where beginnings and endings are relevant. The Immortal Reality, and so the Liberated one also, is not bound by time.

गताः कलाः पञ्चदश प्रतिष्ठा देवाश्च सर्वे प्रतिदेवतासु ।
कर्माणि विज्ञानमयश्च आत्मा परेऽव्यये सर्व एकीभवन्ति ।। ७ ।।

gatāḥ kalāḥ pañcadaśa pratiṣṭhā
devāśca sarve prati-devatāsu ।
karmāṇi vijñāna-mayaśca ātmā
pare'vyaye sarva ekībhavanti ।। 7 ।।

The fifteen constituent minute parts
Go to their basic abodes;
All the senses (*devas*) too to their respective deities;
One's deeds and self of the essence of specific consciousness,
All become unified in the Imperishable Supreme.

The Upaniṣads in general conceive of every constituent element of an individuated being as having a corresponding cosmic aspect, both formed of the one substance. According to this concept, all individuating elements on dissolution go back and merge with their corresponding cosmic aspects, only to emerge as yet another individuated form or being. How this happens is delineated in the present verse.

Slightly varied are the two-faced pictures of the constituent elements portrayed in different Upaniṣads. The *Bṛhadāraṇyaka Upaniṣad*, for example, enumerates fourteen in serial order, each succeeding one subtler than the preceding one. As it describes each element and its two faces, it takes care to categorically state that both the faces have the one underlying *Puruṣa* (person), consciousness in essence (*cetomaya*), and immortal in nature (*amṛtamaya*) and that this *Puruṣa* himself is indeed *ātman*, *Brahman*, *amṛtam*. To enumerate:

Cosmic Aspect	*Individuated Aspect*
1. Earth (*pṛthivī*)	Body (*śarīra*)
2. Water (*ap*)	Semen (*retas*)
3. Fire (*agni*)	Word (*vāk*)
4. Air (*vāyu*)	Vital breath (*prāṇa*)
5. Sun (*āditya*)	Eyes (*cakṣuḥ*)
6. Directions of the campass (*dik*)	Ears that hear sounds
7. Moon (*candra*)	Mind (*manas*)
8. Lightning (*vidyut*)	Dreaming mind (*taijasa*)
9. Thunder (*stanayitnu*)	Tonal sound (*souvara-śabda*)
10. Space (*ākāśa*)	Inner space (*hṛdākāśa*)
11. Righteousness (*dharma*)	That which pertains to righteousness (*dhārma*)
12. Truth (*satyam*)	That which pertains to Truth (*sātya*)
13. Human	Man
14. *Ātmā*	*Ātmā*

Though following the same general scheme, the *Aitaraya Upaniṣad* introduces it as the creation story. Self alone was the one Reality that existed in the beginning. Nothing else that could pulsate existed then. The Self thought: "Let me create worlds." It created all the worlds from Itself. It thought then, "Here are the worlds. Now its guardians are needed." From water He created the cosmic Person (*Puruṣa*). Upon him

He brooded and as a result were separated out his various organs, and from each of them emerged a different cosmic element. These elements finally entered a human form and became its organs, corresponding to the cosmic person's organ whence each emerged. From the cosmic person's mouth, for example, emerged speech and from that speech the cosmic element fire emerged. Finally this fire entered the mouth of the human being and became his speech. The constituent factors detailed in the *Aitaraya Upaniṣad* could be put into a chart as follows:

	Cosmic person's organ	*Cosmic person's function*	*Corresponding element in the cosmos*	*Corresponding organ in the human form*
1.	Mouth	Speech	Fire	Mouth
2.	Nostrils	*Prāṇa*	Air	Nostrils
3.	Eyes	Sight	Sun	Eyes
4.	Ears	Hearing	Directions	Ears
5.	Skin	Heirlings	Plants and herbs	Skin
6.	Heart	Mind	Moon	Heart
7.	Navel	*Apāna*	Death	Navel
8.	Penis	Semen	Water	Penis

There are many references to this scheme, though not as detailed, in the other Upaniṣads. Even while the going back of the individuated aspects into their respective cosmic aspects and the eventual re-emergence of new individuated entities go on unhindered, the original Substance in them, the Self, remains unaffected, Its creative self-expression as all individuated and cosmic aspects goes on unhindered. The difference from text to text on this issue is chiefly in regard to the number of constituent elements (*kalās*), which according to the present Upaniṣad is fifteen. Though reference to these fifteen elements is to be found nowhere else in the Upaniṣads, the *Praśna Upaniṣad* cites the *Puruṣa* or the Self as having sixteen *kalās*, the number nearest to the present one, and Śaṅkara therefore thinks both references connote the same scheme. Yet, while referring to the sixteen *kalās* as pertaining to the non-dual *Puruṣa* or the Self, the *Praśna Upaniṣad* makes no mention of their individual and cosmic aspects.

The nature and number of categories identified in a particular context depend generally on the nature of the context concerned. The Indian medical science of *Āyurveda*, for example, conceives the physical body as being constituted of seven basic elements called *dhātus*. Tallying the number of constituent elements, therefore, is not what matters. What is of import in the present context is that each factor in an individual being has a corresponding factor in the cosmic system — both one substance in essence —and that on dissolution the individual facets get merged into their related cosmic facets, — for example, speech into fire, *prāṇa* into air, and so on.

Likewise, senses are still subtler factors of individual beings. They too, at dissolution, go back to and merge into their universal counterparts, referred to here as *devatās* (*deities*), literally, universal effulgent factors.

The ability to perform deeds (*karmas*), whether physical, mental or verbal, derives from the one transcendental Reality as part of the cosmic system, and therefore, at dissolution they of necessity return to that Reality.

Each is conscious of one's own identity as 'I' — the specific consciousness called here *vijñānātmā* — which also becomes one with the Imperishable Reality, the Self.

Whether looked at as an indivisible individual entity or as its constituent elements, what happens on dissolution, that which we call the death of an individual, is that it becomes merged with the universal. Mere transformation of beingness, death, thus is not the termination of being. Itself imperishable, what really exists continues to exist. The emergence of individual entities from that Reality and their dissolution into Itself are all different facets of one incessant creative self-expression of the One Self.

यथा नद्यः स्यन्दमानाः समुद्रेऽस्तं गच्छन्ति नामरूपे विहाय ।
तथा विद्वान् नामरूपाद्विमुक्तः परात्परं पुरुषमुपैति दिव्यम् ॥ ८ ॥

yathā nadyaḥ syandamānāḥ samudre
astaṁ gacchanti nāmarūpe vihāya ।
tathā vidvān nāma-rūpād-vimuktaḥ
parāt-paraṁ puruṣam upaiti divyam ॥ 8 ॥

As flowing rivers, casting off their names and forms, disappear in the ocean, even so does the awakened one, freed from name and form, attain the effulgent *Puruṣa*, higher than the highest.

स यो ह वै तत् परमं ब्रह्म वेद ब्रह्मैव भवति नास्याब्रह्मवित् कुले भवति ।
तरति शोकं तरति पाप्मानं गुहाग्रन्थिभ्यो विमुक्तोऽमृतो भवति ॥ ९ ॥

sa yo ha vai tat paramaṁ brahma veda
brahmaiva bhavati n'āsy'ābrahmavit kule bhavati ।
tarati śokaṁ tarati pāpmānaṁ
guhā-granthibhyo vimukto'mṛto bhavati ॥ 9 ॥

The knower of Transcendental *Brahman*
Becomes *Brahman* indeed.
In his line is never born a non-*Brahman*-knower.
He, crossing over sorrows
Crossing over sins,
Becomes freed from all knots of heart.
He becomes Immortal.

The famous Upaniṣadic dictum, *brahmaveda brahmaiva bhavati* (the *Brahman*-knower becomes *Brahman* indeed) appears here. A *Brahman*-knower is not merely a knowledgeable person on Brahman; he finds his identity with *Brahman* even as a piece of gold-ornament, on knowing the real content in itself, finds its identity with gold. An awareness, a sense of identity experienced in the here and now while living, it is not a liberation (*mokṣa* or *mukti*) yet to be attained in an unknown future after death. Seeing himself as the Immortal Self, the *Brahman*-knower cannot consider himself to be time-bound, and thus the states before and after the so-called death are not a matter of concern for him.

This wisdom, as an incipient memory factor, passes on to posterity from the enlightened one. The 'line' of posterity (*kula*) understood here need not necessarily be a family one in the biological sense; it could just as well, or even better, be a *guru*-disciple line. A *guru,* never differentiates his biological children from his spiritual children.

Wisdom attained, one overcomes not only sin but also merit, as sin is always accompanied by merit as its counterpart. Transcending merit is not usually experienced as necessary, it is sin alone that worries man; but the enlightened one, the only one who transcends sin absolutely, really goes beyond both.

तदेतदृचाभ्युक्तम् —
क्रियावन्तः श्रोत्रिया ब्रह्मनिष्ठाः स्वयं जुह्वत एकर्षिं श्रद्धयन्तः ।
तेषामेवैतां ब्रह्मविद्यां वदेत शिरोव्रतं विधिवद् यैस्तु चीर्णम् ॥ १० ॥

tadetad-ṛcābhyuktam—
kriyāvantaḥ śrotriyā brahma-niṣṭhāḥ
svayaṁ juhvata ekarṣiṁ śraddhayantaḥ ।
teṣām evaitāṁ brahma-vidyāṁ vadeta
śiro-vrataṁ vidhivad yaistu cīrṇam ॥ 10 ॥

Concerning this very teaching is it
declared in a Ṛgvedic verse:
Those who practise what they learn,
Well versed in scriptures,
Those intent on *Brahman* to the exclusion of all else,
Who make oblation of themselves
To the sole seer with full faith,
To them alone is to be imparted
This secret *Brahman*-wisdom,
When the head-related-rites have been
Duly performed as per injunctions.

Śirovrata (head-related-rite) is a vow enjoined in the *Atharvaveda*, where what is important is holding fire on one's head. The present *śirovrata* is a Vedāntically revised version of that Vedic one. Head is the topmost limb of a human figure both physically and as the centre of attraction of bodily beauty. There is no end to the care mankind lavishes on this one limb to make it as attractive as possible, particularly to the opposite sex. Not to be obsessed with one's physical beauty is a vow observed by seekers as a spiritual discipline, shaving off their hair and beard or letting them grow being a part of this.

Ekarṣi (the sole seer), likewise, is another revised version of a Vedic concept. Vedism enjoins constant kindling of a sacrificial fire known as *ekarṣi,* but in the wisdom context it gains a new dimension, as in the *Īśa Upaniṣad* where it is equated with *Brahman* in Its capacity as the all-seeing Reality, *eka* meaning sole, and *ṛṣi*, seer. The *ekarṣi* rite acceptable to Vedānta is thus one where one offers oneself with full faith (*śraddhā*) as an oblation at the altar-fire of *Brahman*.

Evidently this verse precautions against imparting this secret and sacred wisdom to any incompetent person in any improper way. A wisdom not to be proclaimed in the market-place, meant only for the final liberation of the intent seeker, it is to be the taught to select competent seekers by enlightened masters in its own proper way and handed down thus to posterity, as was seen at the beginning of this very Upaniṣad.

तदेतत् सत्यमृषिरङ्गिराः पुरोवाच नैतदचीर्णव्रतोऽधीते ।
नमः परमऋषिभ्यो नमः परमऋषिभ्यः ।। ११ ।।

tad etat satyaṁ ṛṣir aṅgirāḥ purovāca
naitad acīrṇa-vrato'dhite ।
namaḥ parama-ṛṣibhyo namaḥ parama-ṛṣibhyaḥ ।। 11 ।।

This Truth, being such,
Was declared in olden days
By the seer Aṅgiras.
None of unobserved vows is to read this.
Adoration to the Supreme Seers!
Adoration to the Supreme Seers!

It was as Aṅgiras' answer to Śaunka's question, "Knowing what does all the world become known?" that this Upaniṣad was composed. Aṅgiras got this wisdom from Satyavaha, who in turn got it from Aṅgiran, who got it from Atharvan, and Atharvan from *Brahmā*, the Creator, suggesting that this wisdom has existed ever since the beginning of the world. Known only to a handful of seers, it is not meant to be taught to all. The teaching ends with the warning that this secret widom is to be imparted to none but those whose competence is evident in their practical life. A suggestion that the upkeep of this lineage is the natural moral responsibility of those who benefit from this text, and a like injunction could be read into the lines of this verse.

Salutations to all the seers who kept up this wisdom heritage to our own benefit!

AUM

PEACE INVOCATION

ॐ भद्रं कर्णेभिः शृणुयाम देवा
भद्रं पश्येमाक्षभिर्यजत्राः ।
स्थिरैरङ्गैस्तुष्टुवाँसस्तनूभिर् व्यशेम देवहितं यदायुः ।।

स्वस्ति न इन्द्रो वृद्धश्रवाः स्वस्ति नः पूषा विश्ववेदाः।
स्वस्ति नस्ताक्ष्र्यो अरिष्टनेमिः स्वस्ति नो बृहस्पतिर्दधातु ।।
ॐ शान्तिः । शान्तिः । शान्तिः ।।

oṁ bhadraṁ karṇebhiḥ śṛṇuyāma devā
bhadraṁ paśyema akṣabhir yajatrāḥ ।
sthirair aṅgais tuṣṭuvāṁsastanūbir vyaśema devahitaṁ yad āyuḥ ।।

svasti na indro vṛddhaśravāḥ svasti naḥ pūṣā viśvavedāḥ ।
svasti nastārkṣyo ariṣṭanemiḥ
svasti no bṛhaspatir dadhātu ।।

oṁ śāntiḥ! śāntiḥ! śāntiḥ!

Glossary

Ākāśa: Space. That which gives room for everything to exist. Also called *vyoman*.

Akṣaram: The imperishable. Refers to the Ultimate Reality, *Brahman*.

Ānanda (*ānandam*): Bliss. To be understood in the context of the Good in Western philosophy as a supreme value. *Sat, Cit* and *Ānanda* are terms conjointly used to describe the Absolute (*Brahman*) in Vedānta. Concerning an individual being, it is to be understood as the value consciousness that enables one to evalute one's own experiences either as pleasant or unpleasant.

Anna (*annam*): Food. That which could be enjoyed. Somthing is called *annam* because it is eaten and it eats beings. Even wisdom could be conceived as a sort or food.

Aṇu: Atom. Literally, the indivisible.

Anya: The other. That kind of knowledge which cognizes multiple appearances.

Amr̥ta: Immortality or the Immortal Reality. Poetically imagined as the elixir in a golden pot that emerged from the milk ocean when the *deva*s and the *asura*s churned it together.

Aparā vidyā: Worldly knowledge, aimed at worldly gains. Represented by Vedism in the present Upaniṣad.

Apauruṣeya: Of non-human origin. Vedas are considered so.

Āraṇyaka: A section of Vedic literature. Literally, that which is related to forests.

Arcir-mārga: See *Devayāna*.

Asat: See *sad-bhāva.*

Ātma (*ātman*): The self (from the root *āt* to pervade). The invisible reality or stuff that pervades any visible form. Often confused with *jīva*, the soul. Used in slightly altered senses according to the context. The simplest meaning of the word is 'I' or 'oneself'.

Ātma-vidyā: Self-knowledge.

Bhaikṣacarya: The way of living on alms.

Bhāva: Becoming. Any manifest form of that which exists (*sat*). Derived from the root *bhū* 'to become'.

Brahma: The creater. One of the trinities of the Indian pantheon.

Bhūloka: The earth: *bhū,* the earth; *loka,* world.

Brahmacārin (from *Brahman*, the Absolute, and *cārin*, one who move on). One who is moving on the path of *Brahman*. Name of one who is in the first stage of life as a student in a *gurukula*. Such a way of life is called *brhmacarya*. As a corollary, this kind of life would include such disciplines as continence as helpful to realization. But sex is only one of the implied considerations in the discipline of *brahmacarya*. As evidenced many times in the Upaniṣads, *r̥ṣis* have been married and still able to walk the path of *Brahman.*

Brahman: The Absolute. Derived from the root *br̥h*, to grow constantly. Literally, that which grows constantly.

Brahma-vidyā: The science of the Absolute. Another name for Vedānta.

Cit: Literally, consciousness. The essential content of the imperishable Reality pervading all the perishable and visible forms is pure consciousness. Hence, *Brahman* is disignated as *cit*. See *sat* and *ānanda* also.

Cidākāśa: The consciousness-space.

Dava (*devas*): Gods. Inhabitants of Vedic heaven.

Deva-yāna: The path of the gods. One of the two paths through which the departed souls supposedly go to the other world from where they will not return. Literally, the bright path. Also called *śukla-gati*, the white path. See *pitr̥-yāna*.

Dhīra: Brave, bold, courageous. Etymologically, one who imparts knowledge.

Dhūma-mārga: See *pitr̥-yāna*.

Gauṇa: That which is related to qualities (*guṇa*s). The power of words to be meaningful, especially in the Vedic context.

Guru: (from *gu* darkness, and *ru* to counteract). The banisher of darkness or ignorance. A spiritual teacher or preceptor.

Hr̥t, hr̥daya: Heart.

Kalā: A minute part of anything. Also means, art.

Karma: All actions in general. Philosophically the creative urge inherent in the Imperishable Reality, causing the emergence of all manifest forms. In the Vedic context the ritual of burnt sacrifice enjoined by the Vedas. As a religious belief of the Hindus, the incipient memory factors clinging on to the souls as a result of their deeds in previous births. All are bound to enjoy or suffer the fruits of their deeds, and will have to reincarnate for this purpose. One might be accumulating more *karma*s in the new birth. This vicious chain of action goes on till one attains final release. Such *karma*s are divided into three categories *sañcita-karma* (the actions accumlated in all the previous births), *āgāmi-karma* fresh actions to be done in the present lifetime) and *prārabdha-karma* (actions already initiated but the eating of their fruits is not finished with).

Karma-mārga: The way of actions. The path of rituals.

Karma-yoga: The *yoga* of action. Realizing one's oneness with total existence by performing deeds with the awareness that all actions belong to the total nature, not to any individual being.

Kṛta: That which is done.

Kṣetra-kṣetrajña: The field and the knower of the field. *Kṣetra*, difined as body in the *Bhagavad Gītā*, includes in it everything that is changeful, both physical and mental. *Kṣetrajña* is the consciousness that witnessess all that happens in the realm of *kṣetra*. The entire Chapter XIII of the *Bhagavad Gītā* is devoted to a discussion of this, one of the central problems of philosophy.

Īśa (*Īśvara*): The Sanskrit equivalent to God. Literally, one who controls. It refers to the principle that controls the integral law that sustains each entity as a particular mode of expression of the universal being.

Iṣṭa-karma: Vedic rituals such as burnt sacrifices. One of the two kinds of meritorious deeds. See *pūrta-karma*.

Itihāsa: The Sanskrit word for 'epic'. Defined as the narration of ancient historical events in order to teach the four basic human values, viz., *dharma* (righteousness), *artha* (welth), *kāma* (desire, erotics) and *mokṣa* (final liberation).

Japa: Muttering of holy words. The clarity of muttering is to be accompanied by the clarity of its meaning in the mind.

Jīva: The Sanskrit equivalent to 'soul'. Literally, a being that sustains through breathing. Often confused with *ātmā*, the self.

Jñāna-mārga: The way of wisdom, taught mainly by Upaniṣads.

Jñānin (*jñānī*): One who possesses *jñāna*. One who has attained enlightenmet. *Jñāna* means Wisdom as contrasted with *karma* (works or ritulas). *Jñāna-mārga* or the way of Wisdom gives primacy to reason and intuition.

Loka: The world. That which could be looked at.

Manana: See *Nididhyāsana*.

Mantra: Any stanza of Vedic hymns. Literally, those words which save the person who contemplates them. Also meant to be chanted beautifully. The ritualistic part of the Vedas.

Manuṣya: Man; humankind. Literally the decendents of Manu, the thinking being.

Māyā: Connotes a factor of epistemological and methodological importance in Śaṅkara's Vedānta especially, and in the Upaniṣadic lore generally. Whatever is postulated as the cause of the unreal, spoken of in the most generic of categorical terms in philosophy, as against theology, is to be laid at the door of *māyā.* It is the basis of duality or synergic antinomies. The nearset Western equivalent is the *Nagativitat* of Hegel's system.

Martya: Man. Literally, one destined to die.

Mukti (*mokṣa*): Final liberation. Literally, 'freedom'.

Mūrta: That which is concrete as against abstract. That which has distinct perceivable qualities.

Nididhyāsana: The last stage of gaining wisom. *Śravaṇa* (hearing the word of instruction from the *guru*) and *manana* (intense cogitation on what is heard from the *guru*) are the two stage preceding.

Nirveda: Sense of detachment.

Nirviśeṣa: That which has no qualities.

Nivṛtti-mārga: The way of withdrawal. See *pravṛtti-mārga*. Followed by those who are interested in wisdom.

Pañcāgni-vidyā: The science of five fires. Knowledge concerning five sacrificial fires maintained by orthodox Hindus, namely, *Dakṣiṇāgni, Gārhapatyāgni, Āhavanīyāgni, Sabhyāgni, Āvasatāgni*. It gains a revised dimension in Vedānta.

Para-vidyā: Transcendental knowledge. The supreme wisdom represented by the Upaniṣads.

Parihāra-karma: Expiatory rituals.

Prakr̥ti: Nature. Literally, that which is always in an active state. This activeness is inherent in the ultimate Reality or *Brahman*. *Brahman* in an active state is called *prakr̥ti*.

Prāṇa: The vital breath. The functions of vital breath are identified as five, namely *prāṇa* (going upward), *apāna* (going downward), *vyāna* (that which takes vitality to every part of the body), a *samāna* (that which keeps the balance of the body) and *udāna* (that which leaves the body at death).

Praṇava: Another word for *auṁ*. Literally 'the ever new'.

Pitr̥-yāna: The path of the manes. One of the two paths through which the departed souls are supposed to travel to the other world from where they would have to return. Also called *kr̥ṣṇa-gati*, the black path. See *Deva-yāna*.

Pravacana: Discourse given by a learned person or a *guru*. After completing formal education under a *guru*, a student has to continue his studies at home through self-study (*svādhyāya*) complemented by attending to discourses of the learned as and when occasion arises. Eventually he too will have to give discourses.

Pravr̥tti-mārga: The way of active involvement. See *Nivr̥tti-mārga*.

Pūjā: Worship.

Purāṇa: Literally, the ancient. The collection of Indian legends.

Pūrta-karma: Any act of pious liberality, such as digging public wells, planting shade trees, building camp sheds for travellers. One of the two kinds meritorious deeds.

Puruṣa: Literally, 'person'. The word is used both in the univesal and particular senses. In the universal sense, He is the cosmic person who has the entire cosmos for his body. In this sense He is often called *virāt puruṣa*.

Rasa: Essence, juice, aesthetic enjoyment.

R̥ṣi: A Seer. A wise sage of ancient India who lived generally in the seclusion of forests. They wrote all the hymns of the Vedas as well as the Upaniṣads. They were not necessarily monks and many of them had families.

Sādhana-catuṣṭaya: The common name of the four principal prerequisite qualifications of a seeker. They are *nitya-anitya-vastu-viveka* (discrimination of the eternal and transient values), *vairāgya* (sense of detachmant towards transient values), the six disciplines beginning with *sama* and *mumukṣutva*. The six disciplines are *śama, dama, uparati, titikṣa, śraddhā samādhānam* (See *Śama*).

Śama: Checking the mind and turning it away from distractions. One of the six qualities to be developed by self-effort as part of the spiritual discipline. The other five are *dama* (self-restraint by withdrawing sense-organs from their objects), *uparati* (non-dependence on the extenal), *titikṣa* (endurance), *śraddhā* (full faith in the words of one's *guru* and of the scriptures) and *samādhāna* (having the thought of *Brahman* always in mind).

Saṁhitā: Literally, that which is conjoined inseparably. Name of the initial part of the Vedas, dealing mainly with rituals. Also called *mantra.*

Saṁsāra: Worldly life that passes through a succession of states causing sufferings. Often considered as an ocean. Transmigration of souls is also considered part of it.

Śānti: Peacefulness. The one goal all aim at.

Saṁnyāsa: To renounce all worldly possessions, attachments and positions.

Saṁnyāsin: Renunciate. Monk. One who has given up all worldly possessions and relations.

Sapta-jihvā: A name of fire. Literally, the seven-tongued.

Śarīra: Literally that which perishes. The physical body or the visible form.

Saviśeṣa: Anything understood as having differentiating qualities.

Śāstra: Literally, science. Any basic scripture.

Sat: That which exists always. The subsisting reality in all the transient forms of the visible world, even as gold is the subsisting reality in all ornaments. *Brahman* as this subsisting Reality is designated as *sat*. See *Ānanda* and *Cit* also.

Satyam: Reality, Truth, the truthful way of living.

Śiṣya: A disciple-seeker.

Smṛti: Learning or scriptural lore remembered by a student when he applies pure wisdom-teachings to his practical life. Obligatory conduct and works of religious duty belong to this catagory. Also known as *Dharma Śāstra*. What is taught in them are subject to alterations in accordance with time and clime.

Śraddhā: One of the prerequisites on the part of a seeker. Willingness to have full faith in the truthfulness of the word of the *guru* and of the scriptures. A necessary stepping stone for *manana*. (See *Manana*).

Śravaṇa: See *Nididhyāsana*.

Śruti: That which is heard. The words heard from a *guru*. The recorded writings of *guru* is concerning pure wisdom teaching. All the Upaniṣads are considered *śruti*s. What is taught in the *śruti*s is of eternal value, as against those of *smṛti*s.

Sūkṣma-śarīra: Subtle body. A concept brought into Vedānta by Śaṅkara.

Tapas: Austere self-discipline. Literally, heating up.

Tattva-darśin: A real philosopher. Literally, One who perceives oneself as That.

Tat tvam asi: That thou art. One of the great dicta of Vedānta.

Vairāgya: Sense of detachment towards everything transient.

Veda (*Veda*s): The earliest of the Indian scriptures, collected into four volumes, named the *Ṛgveda, Yajurveda, Sāmaveda* and *Adharvaveda*. They praise gods like Indra, Varuṇa, Mitra and other phenomenal gods of nature.

They were later overcome by the Upaniṣads. The word *veda* means knowledge. The Vedas generally stand for rituals (*karma*).

Vidhi: Injunction, particularly Vedic injunction.

Vidvān: The learned.

Virāṭ-puruṣa: See *Puruṣa*.

Viśva: The cosmos. Literally, 'the all'.

Viśva vīrya: Cosmic creative urge. Equivalent to the *elan vital*.

Upādhi: Conditioning factors that make indistinct Reality appear in distinct forms.

Upaniṣad: Wisdom texts appended to the Vedas. Also called Vedānta as it appears at the end of the Vedas, and *jñāna-kāṇḍa* as it deals with wisdom. The word literally means 'to sit nearby and below' (*upa* = just below, *ni* = nearly, *sat* = to sit down). The name indicates a disciple sitting beside a *guru*. The word also means, 'the secret teaching'. The Upaniṣads teach the philosophy of *Brahman*, the Absolute. The ten major Upaniṣads are *Īśa, Kena, Kaṭha, Praśna, Muṇḍaka, Māṇḍūkya, Taittirīya, Aitareya, Chāndogya* and *Bṛhadāraṇyaka.*

Upāsanā: Worshipping or mediating. Literally, to sit down nearly and do service.

Yajña: Any sacrificial offering.

Yogī (*Yogin*): One who is adept in Yoga.

Index